A Special Creation

FIRST PRINTING

Billy Crone

Cover Design:
CHRIS TAYLOR

To my son, Billy.

When the news of your soon arrival came,
I remember praying to God with this concern.
"How can I share a father's love with two children equally?"
Your sister had already filled my heart.
Could there be room for another?

And lo and behold our Heavenly Father
did what only He could do.
He increased my heart with even more love
than I ever thought imaginable.
And now I have twice the love and double the joy
from two wonderful children
who truly are equally precious to me.

You are my only son and therefore,
we not only share a common heritage,
but first and last names as well.
They mean guardian and crown.

It is my prayer and greatest desire,
that one day you join your mother and I
in guarding the faith that was entrusted to us
and hopefully laying down several crowns
at the feet of Jesus Christ
from Whom one day every knee shall bow
and tongue confess that He is Lord over all.

I share these truths with you,
as an aid in this highest of all callings.
Join us my son.
Come, fight the good fight,
Defend the truth, the only truth
both now and forevermore.

We love you Billy.

Contents

PART 4:   **In the Days of Noah**

PART 5:   **The Truth about Dinosaurs**

Preface

Even though the teachings of evolution clearly undermine the teachings of the Bible, starting from page one, the Genesis account, many Christians still persist in not seeing the absolute utter importance of defending the authority, accuracy, and integrity of the Biblical account in our culture today. This behavior is not only shocking; it simply flies in the face of what the Bible clearly says we should be doing as Christians.

1 Peter 3:15 "Always being ready to make a defense to everyone who asks you to give an account for the hope that is in you."

Notice how the Apostle Peter says that we are to not just defend, but we are to "always" be ready to do so to "everyone." So if the teachings of evolution are being thrust upon "everyone" and are "always" contradicting the hope that is in us, where then are the Christians who are "always" defending it? Do you see the obvious dilemma here? Furthermore, to add insult to injury, neither does the bulk of Christianity seem to realize what another great Apostle, the Apostle Paul, clearly understood so long ago; that the Biblical account of creation is one of the greatest ways to share the good news of the Gospel with the non-Christian.

Acts 17:22-27 "So Paul stood in the midst of the Areopagus and said, Men of Athens, I observe that you are very religious in all respects. For while I was passing through and examining the objects of your worship, I also found an altar with this inscription, TO AN UNKNOWN GOD Therefore what you worship in ignorance, this I proclaim to you. The God who made the world and all things in it, since He is Lord of heaven and earth, does not dwell in temples made with hands; nor is He served by human hands, as though He needed anything, since He Himself gives to all people life and breath and all things; and He made from one man every nation of mankind to live on all the face of the earth, having determined their appointed times and the boundaries of their habitation, that they would seek God, if perhaps they might grope for Him and find Him, though He is not far from each one of us."

Now, notice how the Apostle Paul didn't even mention one verse of Scripture when he preached to the pagans in Athens. Not that quoting Scripture is bad, it's not. It's very good. But Paul's technique if you will was to simply tell them about the Biblical account of creation. That there really is a Creator God who made all of life, including us, and that He's really not that far from us if we would only look. Later, the passage proceeds to tell us that some of the people responded and were actually saved. Why? Simply because the Apostle Paul used and shared the witness of creation. Oh, that we Christians would stop being disobedient to God and disinterested towards the lost. Life is not a game people. All eternity hangs in the balance. Maybe you've got your fire insurance, but others do not. Therefore, may this book not only equip and encourage you in the Biblical account of God's creation and the authority of His Word, but may it cause you to realize the importance and power of the witness of creation and motivate you to share it like the Apostle Paul did with others so they might be saved before it's too late.

One last piece of advice. When you are through reading this book then will you please READ YOUR BIBLE? I mean that in the nicest possible way. Enjoy and I'm looking forward to seeing you someday!

Billy Crone
Las Vegas, Nevada
2017

Part III

A Special Creation

Chapter Seventeen

The Lie of the Ape Men

Until the 1990's no trial in American history attracted more attention than this one did. It was held in 1925 in Dayton, Tennessee and it accused a teacher of violating a state law that banned the teaching of human evolution.

Although the teacher had not taught biology and could not even remember for sure whether he'd discussed evolution while substituting for the regular teacher, he agreed to be arrested and stand trial anyway.

For the contest, the ACLU brought in several big-city attorneys, including the famed criminal lawyer and atheist Clarence Darrow from Chicago. And to assist the prosecution, the World's Christian Fundamentals Association secured the services of William Jennings Bryan of Nebraska, a three times candidate for president and antievolutionist.

It was until this trial that most public schools taught the divine creation theory. Students in those days studied the facts of science and were told that the evidence indicates there is a Creator who designed the universe and plants and animals. But that was soon to change.

The trial lasted eight days and as expected, it ended in a conviction for the young teacher, whose own attorneys even conceded his guilt.

However, in that famous trial, atheist lawyer Clarence Darrow said, 'It is bigotry to only teach *one view of origin.*' He said, 'Students should be taught both the creation and evolution theories.'

So in the 35 years following that trial, the theory of evolution was not only taught more and more, but it was being presented as if it were a proven scientific fact. Until today, we actually have this trial in reverse. Evolution is now the only theory that is taught.

Of course, I'm talking about the infamous 'Scopes Monkey Trial.'[1]

Now how many of you guys have ever heard about The Scopes Monkey Trial before? Yeah, I'm sure most of us have. But what most of us don't know about The Scopes Monkey Trial is that it seemed to be a watershed event that forever changed our nation. How do I know? Because even though evolutionists lost that famous case, a momentum for evolutionary teachings began to take a foothold. And over the next 35 years, the theory of evolution was taught more and more in our schools. Until finally, in the early sixties, prayer and Bible reading were taken out and evolution was put in. And the results have been disastrous! Let's take a look at the official behavioral statistics from the U.S. Census Bureau from about 1963 on, and you tell me if evolutionary teaching hasn't had a horrible impact on our country.

1. Back in the 1950's, the average textbook only had two to three thousand words about evolution. But in 1963, it jumped up to 33,000 words. And it just so happened that 1963 is also when prayer and Bible reading was taken out of the American school system. Gee, I wonder what affect this had had on our country?

2. Since 1963, sexually transmitted diseases among teenagers and young adults have increased nearly 400%.

3. Instances of pre-marital sex among teenagers have skyrocketed.

4. Unwed pregnancies among young girls are up 553%.

5. Unmarried couples living together are up 725%.

6. Divorce rates are up to 111%. Some parts of California the divorce rate is one for every marriage!

7. Single parent households are quickly becoming the norm.

8. SAT scores have plummeted.

9. Alcohol and drug consumption have gone ballistic!

10. Violent crimes are up 995%.

11. Gee, if you tell kids they came from an ape, then why are we surprised when they act like apes![2]

Now folks, I don't know about you, but I'd say the effects of evolutionary teaching hasn't been very good for our country, how about you? And gee, I guess that's why we need to continue in our study called, "The Witness of Creation." And what we've been doing is taking a look at the five different evidences of creation that God has left behind for us showing us that He's not just real, but that we really can have a personal intimate relationship with Him, the Creator of the universe!

And so far we've seen the first evidence God left behind for us showing us this amazing truth is The Evidence of An Intelligent Creation. And then in the last six chapters we saw the second evidence was A Young Creation. And there we saw how evolution Calls Jesus Christ a Liar, God the Father a Liar and even God's Word a Liar by giving us these huge dates of millions and billions of years for our supposed existence. Therefore, we exposed this lie by looking at the Evidence of Space, the Evidence of Earth, the Evidence of Logic, the Fallacy of Carbon Dating and all other evolutionary dating methods, the Fallacy of the Geologic Column and in the last chapter the Evidence of Rapid Formation of Rocks, Caves, Stalagmites and Stalactites, and even Fossils showing us that we really do have A Young Creation just like the Bible says!

But people, believe it or not, did you know that An Intelligent Creation and A Young Creation are not the only evidences that God has left behind for us showing us that He's not just real, but that we really can have a personal intimate relationship with Him, the Creator of the universe? The **third** evidence He's left behind for us is **A Special Creation**. But don't take my word for it. Let's listen to God's.

Genesis 1:24-28 "And God said, Let the land produce living creatures according to their kinds: livestock, creatures that move along the ground, and wild animals, each according to its kind. And it was so. God made the wild animals according to their kinds, the livestock according to their kinds, and all the creatures that move along the ground according to their kinds. And God saw that it was good. Then God said, Let us make man in our image, in our likeness, and let them rule over the fish of the sea and the birds of the air, over the livestock, over all the earth, and over all the creatures that move along the ground. So God created man in his own image, in the image of God he created him; male and female he created them. God blessed them and said to them, Be fruitful and increase in number; fill the earth and subdue it. Rule over the fish of the sea and the birds of the air and over every living creature that moves on the ground."

Now folks, according to our text, the Bible is clear. After God made the animals, He made who? He made me and you, mankind, right? But not only that, what else did it say? God made mankind specifically in His what? In His image, right? But here's the problem. What does evolution teach? Do they say we were specially created in the image of a special God? No! They say we were created by chance in the image of an ape! They don't say God created us after the animals. They say we actually came from an animal, right? Therefore, I'd say we better take a look at not just the Scriptural evidence but the scientific evidence of this supposed **Ape-Man Evolution** and see who's telling the truth, how about you? But before we do that, let's take a refresher course in the evolutionary answer as to the supposed origin of man. Here's the typical textbook response.

In the beginning, about four billion years ago, the air was unfit to breathe. The earth was without life as the sun beat down, storms lashed the coasts and volcanoes poured hissing lava into the ocean's waters.

But it was these natural jolts that fused simple molecules into more complex ones. Amino acids started to be formed and then interact with each other and soon primitive proteins were fashioned, perhaps as a worm-like molecule.

Somehow the right molecules got together and the first living cell appeared. This first living cell is the great ancestor of all plants and animals on earth, including man. From this first cell, all other forms of life evolved. This tiny first living cell is the father of us all!

How did man come from this first cell? Here's the story. As time went on, this first cell developed into amoeba-like organisms and other primitive creatures that could survive in the ocean.

After millions of years, these creatures evolved into fish. Some of these fish developed lungs so that they could survive outside of the water. Gradually they began to make their way onto land as the first amphibians.

These amphibians then evolved into reptiles and the earth soon became populated with great dinosaurs. Some of these reptiles started to develop legs that could move around better, and these creatures became what we today would call mammals. Other reptiles developed wings and flew away to become birds.

Where did man come from? One of these early mammals was known as a tree shrew. He was not much larger than a squirrel and in many ways looked like a squirrel.

This creature lived in trees and gradually evolved into primitive monkeys and other ape-like creatures. And from these ape-like creatures there evolved the great apes that we can see in zoos today as well as a creature who came down from the trees and started walking upright. THIS IS MAN!

Our father, that first living cell, would have been very proud of us if he could have seen how far we have come these past millions of years![3]

Now folks, how many of you had that typical story drilled in your heads from wee high that we supposedly came from a supposed simple cell, to a blob of gel, to an ape that smells? Of course, it's commonplace, right? But the point is this. Is it really true? Did we really come from an ape? I don't think so! How do I know?

Because the **first reason** why we know we were created in the image of God is **Because the Ape Man Evolution is a Lie**! People we are going to take a look at the supposed accounts of apes evolving into man and you tell me if we haven't been lied to.

Nebraska Man: In 1922, scientists discovered a fossil that was reported to be 1 million years old, and it was heralded as the "missing link" in human evolution. It was called "Nebraska Man" since it was found in the state of Nebraska and Henry Osborn, an eminent paleontologist said it combined characteristics of chimpanzees and man. This fossil became famous because it was used as evidence for evolution in the 1925 Scopes trial. For many years, evolutionists described Nebraska Man as a missing link. But the only problem is that this fossil did not belong to any type of human or ape. It was found to be just a mere tooth and that of a pig! Eager evolutionists built a whole imaginary society and lifestyle around this single tooth! They built the entire Nebraska man out of plaster of Paris and imagination and then they even built him a wife. You have to be good to know what his wife looks like from his tooth!

Piltdown Man: For more than 50 years we were led to believe that this ancient creature was another supposed ancestor of modern man. It was found in a gravel pit in Sussex England in 1912 and was considered by some sources to be the second most important fossil proving the evolution of man. But when two scientists eventually took a closer look, they found out that Piltdown man was actually a fraud. The original discoverers took a human skull and an ape's jaw bone, filed them down and made them fit together, treated them with acid, buried them in a gravel pit and then "discovered" Piltdown man. 500 people studied the fossils and wrote a Ph.D. dissertation and earned a doctors degree on the Piltdown fossils, all based on a fraud! For decades boys and girls went to school and were taught that Piltdown man was proof of evolution and it was a hoax. I wonder how many kids during those years lost confidence in the Bible and never got saved.

Neanderthal Man: This is the first supposed ape-man found in Darwin's day. Still synonymous with brutishness, the first Neanderthal remains were found in 1856, in the Neander Valley of Germany, by a school teacher who discovered a skull cap and a few other bones. Then in 1908, Professor Boule of The Institute of Human Paleontology in Paris declared Neanderthal an ignorant knuckle-dragging ape-like man because of his low eye brow ridges and the stooped over posture. However, upon closer examination, it has been discovered that Neanderthal was just as human as us, and his stooped appearance was because of arthritis and rickets. The Neanderthal skeleton they found was bent over not because he was slowly evolving, slowly coming up. It was an old man with arthritis slowly going down! Expert Rudolf Virchow declared, "The curved leg bones were the result of rickets, a vitamin deficiency, and the knots of bone above the eyes had been caused by damage to the skull." And as far as the low eyebrow ridges and long sloping forehead, we see this same feature in people still alive today. Here's a photo of a Malaysian native with the same skull characteristics. Furthermore, these so-called Neanderthals are now recognized as skilled hunters, believers in an after-life, and even skilled surgeons. But the Neanderthal man is still in textbooks right now, even though it was proven wrong 50 years ago.

Java Man: This supposed prehistoric man was found on the island of Java and was reported to be the missing link between man and ape. It was another one of the first alleged "ape men" ever found and used by evolutionists. This Java man was initially discovered by Dutchman Eugene Dubois in 1891, all that was found was a skullcap, three teeth and a femur. The femur was found 50 feet away from the original skullcap a full year later. But after serious study it was discovered that the two pieces of Java Man were from two different skulls from two different areas of the island. And later on, and after closer study, Eugene Dubois, who made the original discovery, rejected their authenticity and admitted that his fossil findings were the mixing together of human skull remnants and of the femoral bone of a giant gibbon. He must have had a bad conscience.

Peking Man: This supposed manlike creature was found in a cave in Peking China during the early part of this century. No other scientists have directly observed the original site and it has not actually been seen in more than 50 years. Only the skulls of the Peking man were ever found and never the lower skeleton as well a few human-like tools. And what's interesting is that all of the examples of Peking Man had the back of their skulls smashed in, exactly matching the result when people of that region hunt for monkey brains. Monkey meat is very tough and quite difficult to eat, but the interior of monkey skulls even today is considered as a delicacy from some Southeast natives. As it turns out, Peking man represents not man's ancestor but man's meal and the tools were used to bash in the skulls to eat the brains of a monkey.

Ramapithicus: For more than 20 years Ramapithicus was considered as one of man's ancestors on the basis of some teeth and jaw remnants. It is included in millions of textbooks and Time-Life volumes on human evolution. In fact, a detailed reconstruction of his whole body walking upright was constructed, mind you, only from jaws and teeth. And if that wasn't bad enough, fossil findings in Turkey in 1980 and in Pakistan in 1982 proved that Ramapithicus represented extinct kinds of monkeys closely resembling the orangutan.

Orce Man: This creature was found in the southern Spanish town of Orce in 1982, and hailed as the oldest fossilized human remains ever found in Europe. Scientists had said the skull belonged to a 17 year- old man who lived 900,000 to

1.6 million years ago, and even had very detailed drawings done to represent what he would have looked like. But only one year later, officials admitted that the skull fragment was not human but probably came from a 4 month-old monkey.

Lucy: Lucy is the latest find that has been almost universally accepted as mankind's ancestor. Discovered in 1974 at Dar Valley, Ethiopia by Donald Johanson. Lucy was less than half a complete skeleton that he named after the Beetle's song "Lucy in the Sky With Diamonds". However, when the bones were studied by spectrograph, they were found to match a chimpanzee, rather than a man. But that's not all. What scattered bones that were found were assembled from totally different locations. The knee joint that he found was a mile and a half away from the rest of the skeleton and yet it was labeled in *National Geographic* as "Lucy's Knee". Donald never corrected them; it was not Lucy's knee found a mile and a half away. Then Donald said, "I think Lucy is becoming a human because the ape has a straight femur, but Lucy's knee is angled to the side like a human's. But any monkey that climbs trees has an angled femur and monkeys that walk on the ground have a straight femur. By the way, the St. Louis Zoo put up a display of Lucy with human feet on it. And guess how many foot bones were found. Zero! Pure propaganda! As it turns out, Lucy is just an unusual monkey and there might even still be some still alive in Sumatra down near Vietnam today.

Toumai Man: "Skull turns the clock back on evolution" read a headline of the Times newspaper on July 11th 2002 following an article on the 10th of July 2002 issue of the prestigious science magazine "Nature" about a new species of archaic human being called the Toumai Man. What they found was a near complete cranium, jawbone and teeth and Nature magazine said it belonged to the oldest human like creature yet discovered, supposedly dating 7 million years old. However, by the 12th of July an article appeared in the Science Nature section of BBC news on-line claiming that the skull wasn't quite what it seemed. It turned out to simply be the remains of a gorilla.

Rhodesia Man: Rhodesia Man was found in what is now Zimbabwe and was considered to be the first early human fossil to be found in Africa. However, paleontologists soon discovered that this creature had undoubtedly suffered from tooth decay and were having a hard time understanding how this disease of civilization could have attacked this supposed prehistoric man. And if that wasn't bad enough, two very odd holes in the side of the skull causing the experts even greater perplexity. In the view of Professor Mair of Berlin they looked like the entry and exit holes of a modern day bullet.[4]

Now folks, I don't know about you, but I'd say based on the evidence we just saw, those Ape-Man Accounts are a bunch of bologna, how about you? In fact, I'd say somebody would have to be a "Neanderthal" to believe them! In fact, not only does the evidence we've seen and common sense tell us those Ape-Man accounts are nothing but a bunch of bologna, but believe it or not, even the evolutionists are admitting it. See for yourself.

1. Gareth Nelson of the American Museum of Natural History: "We've got to have some ancestors. We'll pick those. Why? Because we know they have to be there, and these are the best candidates. That's by and large the way it has worked. I am not exaggerating."

2. Anthropologist E.A. Hooten: "From a Neanderthal skull an artist can fashion the features of a chimpanzee or a philosopher and it is wise to not put your faith in reconstructions."

3. John T. Bonner: "We evolutionists have been telling our students for years not to accept any statement on its face value but to examine the evidence, and, therefore, it is rather a shock to discover that we have failed to follow our own sound advice."

4. Miles Eldredge: "We Paleontologists have said that the history of life supports the story of gradual adaptive change, all the while really knowing that it does not."

5. Lord Solly Zuckerman: "The record of reckless speculation of human origins is so astonishing that it is legitimate to ask whether much science is yet to be found in this field at all."

6. T.L. Moor: "The more one studies paleontology, the more certain one becomes that evolution is based on faith alone."

7. Dr. Robert Martin, Zoological Society of London: "In recent years several authors have written popular books on human origins which were based more on fantasy and subjectivity than on fact and objectivity. At the moment science cannot offer a full answer on the origin of humanity."

8. Lord Zuckerman, British Anatomist: "If man evolved from apelike creature there is not even a trace of such evidence in the fossil record."

9. Anthropologist Dr. Lyall Watson: "Modern apes, for instance, seem to have sprung from out of nowhere. They have no yesterday, no fossil record. And the true origin of modern humans – of upright, naked, tool-making, big brained beings – is, if we are honest with ourselves, an equally mysterious matter."

10. Anthropologist Dr. Tim White: "The problem with a lot of anthropologists is that they want so much to find a hominid that any scrap of bone becomes a hominid bone."[5]

Now folks, I don't know about you, but I'd say if the evolutionists are admitting that these Ape-Man accounts are a bunch of bologna, then these Ape-Man accounts must be a bunch of bologna, how about you? And as one guy said, "If all you have is lies to support your theory, then maybe it's time to get a new theory." Hello!

But remember folks, we're not just dealing with a deceptive theory here. We're dealing with the dangerous side-affects of this theory. Again, if you teach kids they came from an ape, why are we shocked when they act like apes! And apparently, that's why Martin Luther warned us of this!

"I am much afraid that the schools will prove to be the great gates to hell unless they diligently labor in explaining the Scriptures, engraving them in the hearts of youth. I advise no one to place his child where the Scriptures do not reign paramount. Every institution in which men are not increasingly occupied with the Word of God, must become corrupt."[6]

Now folks, how many of you would say we are suffering the consequences of not listening to great advice like that? And here's the point. And to think the whole time, it's all based on a pack of lies!

But you might be thinking, "Okay so maybe the supposed evolutionary transition of an ape into a man is a bunch of bologna, but what about the supposed evolution of animals? You know, like the horse and whale, and what about natural selection and mutations and all that other stuff they use to explain how other forms of life supposedly evolved? Well, hey, great question! I guess that's why we'll take a look at that in the next chapter.

Chapter Eighteen

The Lie of Horse & Whale Evolution

Now folks, I don't know if you've noticed or not, but our society today could not only give a rip about what the Bible says, but they even gone so far now as to create their own version of the Bible. For instance, you can now check out the politically correct version where Jesus' being God's only son is now generalized to: "No one knows the Child except the Father-Mother; and no one knows the Father-Mother except the Child."[1] Or maybe you could read the new feminist version where the resurrection passage from Matthew 28 now states, "Mary Magdalene and the other Mary came to see the tomb. But the angel said to the women, 'Do not be afraid, for I know that you seek Judith who was crucified. She is not here; for She is risen.'"[2] And now thanks to evolution, we now have the "new" account of Jesus' birth. Here's a sample:

"He (Jesus) was born in a manger a long time ago, not to a virgin, but to a gorilla. What's so funny? Who did you expect his ancestors to look like, Tom Cruise? But wait. I'm not making fun of Jesus. I'm not mocking religion. In fact, from the deepest wellspring of my heart, I'm despairing something we've lost in our scientific culture.

Yes, if Jesus were alive today, he would understand that his ancestors, just like ours, were beasts. No, he wouldn't run around claiming he was born of a virgin. And, brilliant rabbi that he was, he would likely ask us to understand the miracle stories metaphorically, as morality tales, but certainly not as literal truth."[3]

Hey, folks, it's one thing to make a monkey out of me. But to make a monkey out of my Lord? I don't know about you, but I not only find that statement totally blasphemous, I find it completely ludicrous, especially when we saw in the last chapter how this whole Ape Man Evolution is based on a pack of lies! Oh, but people I'm telling you, that's just the tip of the iceberg and that's precisely why were going to continue in our study, "The Witness of Creation."

In our study so far we've seen the first three evidences of creation that God has left behind for us showing us that He's not just real, but that we really can have a personal intimate relationship with Him, the Creator of the universe was the evidences of An Intelligent Creation from very the Hand of Almighty God, as opposed to blind chance exploding from some sort of primeval blob, and then A Young Creation, as opposed to the long-age fairy tale time of evolution. But in the last chapter we began a new section showing us that the third evidence that God left behind for us was A Special Creation. And there we saw the Bible clearly says we we're created for a special purpose to have a special relationship with a special God, right? But the problem was what evolution teaches. They say we came from a simple cell, to a blob of gel, to an ape that smells, right? Therefore, we took a look at the supposed Ape-Man Evolution with Nebraska man, Piltdown man, Neanderthal man, Java man, Peking man, Ramapithecus, Orce man, Lucy, Toumai man, and finally Rhodesia man. And what we saw in every single case was that they were either a deliberate lie, a hoax, or had nothing at all to do with humans! Liar liar, pants on fire!

But you might be thinking, "Okay so maybe the supposed evolution of an ape into a man is a bunch of bologna, but what about the supposed evolution of **animals**? You know, like the supposed **horse and whale evolution** that evolutionists say proves that animals evolved over millions of years? What about that? Well, hey, great question! But before we look at that, let's get reacquainted with how the Bible says animals came onto the scene.

Genesis 2:19-23 "Now the LORD God had formed out of the ground all the beasts of the field and all the birds of the air. He brought them to the man to see what he would name them; and whatever the man called each living creature, that was its name. So the man gave names to all the livestock, the birds of the air and all the beasts of the field. But for Adam no suitable helper was found. So the LORD God caused the man to fall into a deep sleep; and while he was sleeping, he took one of the man's ribs and closed up the place with flesh. Then the LORD God made a woman from the rib he had taken out of the man, and he brought her to the man. The man said, This is now bone of my bones and flesh of my flesh; she shall be called woman, for she was taken out of man."

Now folks, according to our text, the Bible is clear. As we saw before, God not only made the animals and man on day six, but as we saw here, He specifically brought them to Adam to do what? To name them, right? And ladies, I know we guys can take a while to finish our projects, but how many of you would say it probably didn't take Adam millions and millions of years to name those animals? But not only that, according to our text, neither did it take God millions of years to bring in those animals, did it? I mean, was Adam standing around in line waiting for millions of years for them to evolve? I don't think so! And so here's the obvious problem. Evolution does teach that it took millions and millions of years for them to evolve, right? And once again this is directly opposite to what the Bible says!

Therefore, I'd say we better take a look at not just the Scriptural evidence but the scientific evidence of this supposed **Animal Evolution** and see just whose telling the truth, how about you? But to help us do that, let's first take a refresher course in the evolutionary answer of the supposed origin of animals, starting with the **horse**. Here's the typical textbook response.

Over a period of millions of years the horse grew from being a small fox-like animal that was only about 2 feet tall to the modern-day horse that stands more than 6 feet high. And along it's way it lost all its toes. (I hate it when that happens!) Therefore, the horse did not always look like it does today. In fact, it took about 60 million years for the horse to develop into what we see today.

The first one was called Eohippus, which means, "dawn horse." It was a small forest animal and looked nothing at all like a horse. It had a "doggish" look with an arched back, short neck, short snout, short legs, and a long tail. It probably scampered from thicket to thicket like a modern deer, only stupider, slower, and not as agile. And here's a surprise. A tiger's teeth are mainly pointed and it only eats meat. Well, this first horse also had pointed teeth. So what does this tell us about what it ate? Meat! The first horse was a carnivore. (I wouldn't kick this horse too hard with your spurs…he might eat you!)

Then many millions of years later came Epihippus, Mesohippus, Miohippus, Kalobatippus, Parahippus, Merychippus, Pliohippus, Astrohippus, and Dinohippus each changing along its way until finally today we have our current horse called the Equus. It has completely lost all signs of once having multiple toes and seems to have emerged about 2 million years ago.[4]

Now folks, how many of you were taught or heard that story of horse evolution or maybe even seen it on display somewhere? Of course, it's commonplace, right? But the point is this. Is it really true? Did this animal, the horse, really take millions and millions of years to evolve? I don't think so! Why?

Because the **first reason** why we know God created the animals is **Because this Horse Evolution is a Lie**! People, we're going to take a look at some serious problems with this supposed horse evolution and you tell me if we haven't been lied to.

The Existence Problem: The whole idea of this horse evolution was made up by Othniel Marsh in 1879 and famous evolutionist Thomas Huxley. They produced a diagram, which attempted to show the so-called gradual stages of the horse evolving. The only problem was that Othniel Marsh picked the animals from all over the world. He did not find them in one place and he did not find them in that order. He made the entire thing up! Not only is this supposed order of horse evolution never found in the order it's presented, but there is no one site in the world where the evolutionary succession of the horse can be seen. It doesn't exist!

The Ancient Problem: As it turns out, the supposed first "ancient" horse called Eohippus is not a horse at all. It's called a hyrax and it is still alive today in South America. It's about the size of a fox and is a meat-eating animal with sharp teeth. Then the supposed "ancient" horse called Hipparion which evolutionists say has also been extinct for millions of years is also still alive today. It's called the Okapi and lives in the northeastern rainforests of Zaire in central Africa and is not even a horse or even a relative of the horse. It's a relative of the giraffe.

The Genetic Problem: If the theory of horse evolution were to be true, it has some very serious genetic problems to overcome, such as the ribs, toes, and teeth. In all cases, they are totally different and completely inconsistent. For example, the so-called Eohippus, the ancient horse, had 18 pairs of ribs, the next one had 15 pairs of ribs, the next one after that had 19 pairs, the next one after that had 18 pairs. Then the number of lumbar vertebrae goes from 6 to 8 and then returns to 6 again. What kind of evolution is that?

The Inconsistency Problem: There are more than 20 charts of the evolution of the horse proposed by various researchers and each is totally different from the other. Obviously, even the evolutionists haven't reached a common agreement about this theory.

The Fossil Problem: If the horse evolution were true, you would expect to find the earliest horse fossils in the lowest rock strata. But the problem is, you don't. In fact, bones of the supposed "earliest" horses have been found at or near the surface. Then, some of the supposed three-toed horses have been found with the supposed one-toed horses, showing they lived at the same time. And finally, fossils of modern horse species, the Equus, have been discovered in the same layer as Eohippus, which shows that our modern horse and its supposed ancient ancestor actually lived at the same time.

The Size Problem: The evolutionists assume that the horse has grown progressively in size over millions of years but what they forget is that modern day horses vary enormously in size. The largest horse today is the Clydesdale and the smallest is the Fallabella, which stands only 17 inches tall. Both are members of the same species, and neither has evolved from the other.

The Admission Problem: Evolutionist Boyce Rensberger said, "The popular told example of horse evolution, suggesting a gradual sequence of changes from four-toed fox-sized creatures living nearly 50 million years ago to today's much larger one-toed horse, has long been known to be wrong. Instead of gradual change, fossils of each intermediate species appear fully distinct, persist unchanged, and then become extinct. Transitional forms are unknown."

Then the well-known paleontologist Colin Patterson, a director of the Natural History Museum in London said, "There have been an awful lot of stories, some more imaginative than others, about what the nature of that history of life really is. The most famous example, still on exhibit downstairs, is the exhibit on horse evolution prepared perhaps fifty years ago. That has been presented as the literal truth in textbook after textbook. Now I think that is lamentable, particularly when the people who propose those kinds of stories may themselves be aware of the speculative nature of some of that stuff."

And evolutionist science writer Gordon R. Taylor explains, "But perhaps the most serious weakness of Darwinism is the failure of paleontologists to find convincing phylogenies or sequences of organisms demonstrating major evolutionary change. The horse is often cited as the only fully worked-out example. But the fact is that the line from Eohippus to Equus is very erratic.

Specimens from different sources can be brought together in a convincing-looking sequence, but there is no evidence that they were actually ranged in this order in time."

And evolutionist Prof. Herbert Nilsson said, "The family tree of the horse is beautiful and continuous only in the textbooks. The construction of the whole Cenozoic family tree of the horse is therefore a very artificial one, since it is put together from non-equivalent parts, and cannot therefore be a continuous transformation series."[5]

Now folks, I don't know about you, but I'd say based on the evidence we just saw, somebody's been "horsing around" with the facts, you now what I'm saying? And therefore I'd say this supposed horse evolution is a bunch of bologna, how about you?

Oh, but that's not all. The **second reason** why we know God created the animals is **Because the Whale Evolution is a Lie**! And to show you how big of a lie it really is, let's take a refresher course in the evolutionary answer for origin of the **whale**. Here's the typical textbook response.

Call it an unfinished story but with a plot that's a grabber. It's the tale of an ancient land mammal making its way back to the sea, becoming the forerunner of today's whales. About 50 million years ago its ancestors first learned to swim. You see, whales evolved from warm-blooded, air breathing mammalian ancestors that lived on land. But in doing so, it lost its legs. (I hate it when that happens too!) Then all of its vital systems became adapted to a marine existence, probably in search of food.

First there was Pakicetus and then Ambulocetus, Rodhocetus, Procetus, Kutchicetus, Durodon, Basilosaurus, Aeticetus, Squalodon, Cetotherium, and finally Kentridon. This evolution of the whale from a land mammal was actually the reverse of what happened millions of years ago when the first sea creatures crawled out of the sea and onto the land. Now, some details remain fuzzy and are under investigation. But we know for certain that this back-to-the-water evolution did occur.[6]

Now folks, how many of you were taught or heard that story of whale evolution or maybe even seen it on display somewhere? Of course, it's commonplace, right? But the point is this. Is it really true? Did this animal, the whale, really take millions of years to evolve? I don't think so! Why? Because just like the supposed evolution of the horse, this whale evolution thing has just as many problems. Let's take a look at some serious problems with this theory and you tell me if we haven't been lied to.

The Version Problem: In 1859, Darwin suggested that whales arose from bears, sketching a scenario in which selective pressures might cause bears to evolve into whales. But, embarrassed by criticism, he removed his hypothetical swimming bears from later editions of the *Origin of Species*. Then early in the 20th century, Eberhard Fraas and Charles Andrews suggested that primitive carnivores were the ancestors of whales. Then later, W.D. Matthew of the American Museum of Natural History said whales descended from rat-like creatures, but his idea never gained much support. And then Everhard Johannes Slijper tried to combine the two ideas, claiming that whales descended from a carnivorous rat-like creature. And the current version is that whales evolved from a wolf-like creature. Obviously, the versions are not only different, but also pretty wild!

The Design Problem: Whales and dolphins have many unique features designed to enable them to live in water. For example: They have enormous lung capacity with efficient oxygen exchange for long dives, a powerful tail with large horizontal flukes enabling very strong swimming, eyes designed to see properly in water and able to withstand high pressure, ears designed differently from those of land mammals that pick up airborne sound waves and with the eardrum protected from high pressure, skin lacking hair and sweat glands but incorporating fibrous, fatty blubber, fins and tongues that have counter-current heat exchangers to minimize heat loss, nostrils on the top of the head (blowholes), specially fitting mouth and nipples so babies can be breast-fed underwater, filtering mechanisms for food, and a sonar system which is so precise that it can detect a fish the size of a golf ball 230 feet away.

The obvious question is, "How could this creature "slowly" change from a land dwelling animal with these characteristics? It would have to lose its shaggy hair, its backbone flexibility, its waggly little tail; its nostrils would have had to move from the end of the snout to the top of the head, the long front legs would have had to change into flippers, the back legs would have had to disappear, the external ears would have had to become internal, and the breathing, hearing, and birthing capabilities would have to change from a land based existence to an underwater one. Furthermore all these aquatic features must be fully functional and fully present if the animal is to survive. Therefore, based on the design we see, a gradual step-by-step evolution is not possible.

The Fossil Problem: The only fossil remains of Pakicetus were a skull yet they immediately claimed it was a "primitive whale." However, as it turns out, the fossil had absolutely no connection with the whale and was the remains of a four-footed creature similar to that of a common wolf. Also, it was found in a region full of iron ore, and containing fossils of other land dwelling creatures as snails, tortoises, and crocodiles making it part of a land stratum, not an aquatic one.

The same is true for Ambulocetus, which means, "a walking and swimming whale." First of all, there is absolutely no basis for the claim that it swam in water, or that it lived on land and water like an amphibian. The fossil remains are typical of land-mammal anatomy. Also, major conclusions were made about its mode of walking and about its tail structure, but the important fibula bones, pelvis, and tailbones were not even found. Even more disturbing is the fact that fossils of Ambulocetus were found in strata at or above the levels where modern whale fossils were found.

Then there was Basilosaurus which is Greek for "king lizard." It was actually a serpent-like sea mammal about 70 feet long with a 5-foot long skull. Even though it was 10 times as long as Ambulocetus, evolutionists drew them at the same size to help give the desired "false" impression that they are a genuine transitional series.

Also, Barbara Stahl, a vertebrate paleontologist and evolutionist points out that, "The serpentine form of the body and the peculiar shape of the cheek teeth make it plain that Basilosaurus could not possibly have been the ancestor of modern whales."

The Vestigial Problem: One of the major proofs evolutionists use to say whales evolved from land walking mammals is the supposed vestigial bones that they say were the leftover remains of legs. For example, textbooks often say that the whale has a vestigial pelvis and is evidence of its evolutionary history. Also, a children's book, *Whales & Dolphins* in the first sentence says, "Just imagine whales walking around. It's true." However, those bones are not vestigial nor are they the remains of ancient legs. As it turns out, they are necessary bones that act as an anchor for the muscles of the genetalia and without them the whales cannot reproduce. It has nothing to do with walking on land. It has to do with getting more baby whales.

The Imagination Problem: Evolutionists have made a so-called complete reconstruction of Ambulocetus. However, only a handful of bones were actually found. The actual remains therefore do not include the crucial features needed to support its claim of being a 'transitional' creature between land animals and whales. Or worse yet is the so-called complete reconstruction of Pakicetus, who is supposed to be another alleged transitional form between land animals and whales. The only bones that were found were a couple pieces of a skull. The whole rest of the reconstruction is pure imagination.

The Picture Problem: A similar problem to the imagination problem is the picture problem. A so-called skeletal structure of Pakicetus was published in the Nature magazine. A reconstruction of an upright land walking Pakicetus by Carl Buell, which was based on that structure, was realistic. However, National Geographic portrayed Pakicetus in a swimming position with its hind legs stretching out backwards, and even gave it the impression of having "fins." The problem is, based on the evidence, none of it is true.

Then we have National Geographic's portrayal of Ambulocetus. The animal's rear legs are shown not with feet that would help it to walk, but as fins that would assist it to swim. However, the true leg bones of Ambulocetus possessed the ability to move powerfully on land and are real legs, not "fins." Neither are there any imaginary webs between its toes such as National Geographic added.

The Admission Problem: Evolutionist Robert Carroll said, "It is not possible to identify a sequence of land animals leading directly to whales."

Evolutionist and famous Russian whale expert G.A. Mchedlidze says he does not support the description of Pakicetus, Ambulocetus and similar four-legged creatures as "possible ancestors of the whale," and describes them instead as being a completely isolated group.

And another evolutionary whale expert, E.J. Slijper said, "We do not possess a single fossil of the transitional forms between the aforementioned land animals and the whales."[7]

Now folks, I don't know about you, but I'd say based on the evidence we just saw, somebody's been making up a "whale of a tale," you know what I'm saying? And therefore I'd say this supposed whale evolution is also bunch of bologna, how about you? In fact, based on this kind of track record, I'd say this whole idea of a slow gradual evolution of any kind of animal is also a bunch of bologna!

But you might be thinking, "Okay so maybe the supposed slow gradual evolution of animals like the horse and whale are a bunch of bologna, but what about all the other supposed mechanisms of evolutionary change they come up with? You know, like natural selection and mutations and vestigial organs and all that other stuff they use to explain how life supposedly evolved over millions and millions of years? Well hey, great question! I guess that's why we'll take a look at that in the next chapter!

Chapter Nineteen

The Lie of Natural Selection

Although he was a murderer of millions and master of destruction, he did not come into the world that way. On the evening of April 20th 1889, a boy was born in a small town in Austria. He was the son a customs official named Alois and his third wife named Klara. Initially his father had taken his mother's name, Schicklgruber, but changed it in 1876.

Believe it or not, this young boy regularly attended church services and even sang in the local choir. And although he grew up with a poor record at school and he left before completing, he still had an ambition to become an artist or architect. So to fulfill his dream, he moved to Vienna in 1909 where the Academy of Arts was located.

But to his own surprise he failed to get admission and within a year was living in homeless shelters and eating at charity soup kitchens. So from here he went to Munich and volunteered for service in the army when WWI started in 1914. It was here that he was twice decorated for bravery and rose to the rank of corporal.

Then in 1920, he joined the National Socialist Workers Party and soon became the leader mostly because of his powerful speaking ability. And by 1932, his party became the strongest party so that by 1934, this man had total control of his country. But his desire for domination didn't stop there. By 1939 he invaded Poland, which triggered World War II.

And everything seemed to be going his way until in December 1941 when he assumed personal command of war strategy, which quickly led to disaster. By July 1944, the military situation was so desperate that a group his own people tried to assassinate him but failed. And even though the war was now hopelessly lost by early 1945, this man still insisted that his people fight to the death.

But shortly thereafter, he committed suicide in an underground bunker leaving behind a legacy of one of the most dreadful tyrannies of modern times with more than 11 million people being killed, 6 million of those in gas chambers. In fact, they were exterminated not just for who they were but for what they were. Of course I'm talking about reign of Adolph Hitler.[1]

Now how many of you guys have ever heard about Adolph Hitler and his horrible things he did? Yeah, he's known throughout the world, right? But my point is this. What most of us don't know about Hitler is the reason why he slaughtered millions of people. And folks, believe it or not, his justification came from evolutionary teachings! You see, if Hitler was going to create his master race, then he had to get rid of the lower races, right? And folks it is now known that the reason why he specifically started killing the Jews first was because they were last on his evolutionary scale. Don't believe me? Folks, let's take a look at what's been called Hitler's Hit List and you tell me if it doesn't reek of evolutionary teaching.

Species Blood Mixture

Nordic (blonde, blue eyed)	**Close to pure Aryan**
Germanic (brown hair, blue-eyed or less desirable, brown-eyed)	**Predominately Aryan**
Mediterranean (white but swarthy)	**Slight Aryan preponderance**
Slavic (white but degenerate bone structure)	**Close to Aryan, half-Ape**
Oriental	**Slight Ape preponderance**
Black African	**Predominately Ape**

Jewish (fiendish skull)   **Close to pure Ape**[2]

Now folks, I don't know about you, but I'd say evolutionary teachings are not only a big hoax as we've been seeing, but I'd say they also lead to a big holocaust, how about you? And gee folks, I guess that's why we need to continue in our study called, "The Witness of Creation." And so far we've seen the first three evidences of creation that God has left behind for us showing us that He's not just real, but that we really can have a personal intimate relationship with Him, the Creator of the universe was the evidences of An Intelligent Creation from very the Hand of Almighty God, as opposed to blind chance exploding from some sort of primeval blob, and then A Young Creation, as opposed to the long-age fairy tale time of evolution. And in the last two chapters we've saw how the third evidence was A Special Creation. And so far we've not only seen the supposed ape-man evolution is a bunch of bologna, but in the last chapter we saw the supposed animal evolution is also a bunch a bologna. Why? Well hey, thanks for asking! Because the two best examples they've come up with, the horse and whale evolution, have some serious problems. For instance, the supposed horse evolution had the problems of existence, the ancient problem, the genetic problem, the inconsistency problem, the fossil problem, the size problem and even the admission problem. Then, if that wasn't bad enough, the supposed whale evolution had a version problem, a design problem, a fossil problem, a vestigial problem, an imagination and picture problem, and they too had an admission problem! Therefore, we came to the conclusion that if this is the best they can up with for supposed animal evolution, then any kind of animal evolution is a bunch of bologna!

But you might be thinking, "Okay so maybe this supposed slow gradual evolution of people and animals is a bunch of bologna. But what about all the other supposed mechanisms they come up with, like **natural selection**? Well, hey, great question! But before we look at that, let's once again get reacquainted with the Biblical answer for the existence of animals.

Genesis 6:1-8 "When men began to increase in number on the earth and daughters were born to them, the sons of God saw that the daughters of men were beautiful, and they married any of them they chose. Then the LORD said, My Spirit will not contend with man forever, for he is mortal; his days will be a hundred and twenty years. The Nephilim were on the earth in those days – and also afterward – when the sons of God went to the daughters of men and had children by them. They were the heroes of old, men of renown. The LORD saw how great man's wickedness on the earth had become, and that every inclination of the thoughts of his heart was only evil all the time. The LORD was grieved that he had made man on the earth, and his heart was filled with pain. So the LORD said, I will wipe mankind, whom I have created, from the face of the earth – men and animals, and creatures that move along the ground, and birds of the air – for I am grieved that I have made them. But Noah found favor in the eyes of the LORD."

Now folks, according to our text, the Bible is clear. Out of judgment and grief over mankind's continual wickedness, God not only caused a literal worldwide flood, but He caused it on whom? On the men and animals that He what? That He made, right? But once again, what does evolution teach? Do they say that God's the One Who made animals on the earth? Are you kidding! They say it was natural selection that gave them birth, right? Therefore, I'd say we better take a look at not just the Scriptural evidence but the scientific evidence of this supposed **Natural Selection** thing and see who's telling the truth, how about you? And to help us do that, let's first take a refresher course in how this natural selection thing is supposed to work.

Natural selection, also known as the survival of the fittest, is an idea that was popularized by Charles Darwin. He proposed it as a major driving force behind evolutionary change. However, Darwin actually didn't come up with the idea. He got it from a man named Alfred Wallace who himself was a spiritualist and a Marxist who said the idea of "survival of the fittest" came to him while he was suffering from a fever in Southeast Asia. Afterwards, Wallace wrote back to England, saying that the idea came as an inspiration to him, and that it must be the cause of evolution. It was after this that Charles Darwin stole the idea and published it as his own.

Here's how this "feverish" idea is supposed to work. Those organisms which are best suited to their environment, that is the strongest ones, are the ones most likely to survive and leave behind descendants, hence "survival of the fittest." Therefore, these stronger survivors are said to have a greater chance of passing on their more favorable genes increasingly over generation to generation, while the "less fitted" creatures don't because they lose the struggle to survive over the stronger ones and die or disappear altogether.

Therefore, it is through this "natural" process of nature and this "selection" process of "stronger survivors" that Darwin believed could give rise to totally new traits and totally new creatures indefinitely. In fact, so much was this "stolen" and feverish idea popularized that Sir Julian Huxley boldly stated, "So far as we know, natural selection is the only effective agency of evolution."[3]

Now folks, how many of you ever heard about or were taught this natural selection thing? Of course, it's commonplace, right? But the point is this. Is it really true? Did natural selection really give birth to all the animals we see today? I don't think so! How do I know?

Because the **first reason** why we know God created the animals is **Because Natural Selection is a Lie**! Folks, believe it or not, natural selection is yet another evolutionary hoax! But you might be thinking, "Well gee Pastor Billy, pretty bold to call it a lie. I mean, how do you know?" Well hey, thanks for asking!

The **first reason** why we know Natural Selection is a lie is because **The Process Doesn't Even Work**. People, we're going to take a look at some very serious problems with this natural selection thing and you tell me if we haven't been lied to, yet again!

The Problem of Pre-Existing Traits: Natural selection only "selects" if you will, traits that already exist within a given creature. Therefore, it does not and cannot produce "new" genetic information needed for any "new" organs. And because of this, it cannot lead to the formation of a new kind of species.

The Problem of DNA: The DNA is a wall of which evolution cannot pass across because the DNA code causes a creature to be born like its parents. This is what is called the "*Mendelian laws of heredity*." Now even though the DNA does allow a certain range of variation, the code locks each species into a certain pattern from which it cannot escape. Therefore, DNA is a built in barrier, keeping species from becoming new kinds of creatures altogether.

The Problem Neutral Traits: There are some traits that are neutral, or in other words, they give no benefit to their owner. The logical question is, "How could "neutral" traits have evolved by natural selection, if they offered no selective advantage?" By definition, only the strongest or positive traits should survive?

The Problem of Survival of the Fittest: The very idea of "survival of the fittest" means that creatures who are not fit enough to survive are eliminated. For instance, if a creature is born with features that are too far from the norm, it will not be fit, and it will therefore die. However, this eliminates all extremes and thereby eliminates any hope for evolution to take place. In fact, it would actually make sure the species returns closer to its original pattern, which is precisely what we see in wild plants and animals. All tend to return to the normal. Therefore, "survival of the fittest" produces the opposite of evolution by acting as a conserving force assuring that the species stays the same!

The Problem of Randomness: Not only is natural selection supposed to have produced everything, the process is said to be entirely random. However, all about us we see not randomness but purpose and design in everything. The plant is given roots to extract water and minerals and leaves to process sunlight and water and to produce sugar. Then the animal is given legs, eyes, ears, and marvelous internal organs, all with incredible purpose. Therefore, since nothing is random or haphazard, then the so-called random process of natural selection could never have produced all the non-random or designed structures we see in nature.

The Problem of Limitations: Even if natural selection could provide variations in a creature, variations in creatures have a built in limitation. For instance, farmers have been trying for years and years to breed bigger pigs, but they will never get one as big as a semi will they? Or some insects become resistant to pesticides, but will they ever become resistant to a brick? Therefore, these built in limitations keeps things from becoming a totally new kind of creature.

The Problem of Logic: Again, while we may see many variations within various plants and animal species, they're still the same kind of plant or animal. Therefore, the production of new creatures via natural selection not only never occurs, it's logically impossible.

For instance, how about **almonds**? First they are grown then harvested, hulled, sorted, graded, diced, sliced, slivered, crosscut, split, cubed, chopped, flaked, smoked, roasted, blanched, flavored, pounded into paste, tested and re-tested. And then they're jarred, foil wrapped, canned, bagged, boxed, palletized, bar-coded and stored. Now the question is, "How long would this 'selection process' take to turn those almonds into an Albatross?" Answer: NEVER! This "selection process" of almonds can only produce almonds!

Or how about **rice**? First rice is grown then harvested, and shipped to a processing plant where it will be cleaned, husked and separated with it's thickness graded. Then it will then be whitened, polished, sifted, and it's length measured. Then it's sorted based on color and then sent to be packaged. So the question is, "How long would this 'selection process' take to turn rice into a rhinoceros?" Answer: NEVER! This "selection process" of rice can only produce rice!

Or how about **cattle**? There are well over 200 different breeds of cattle in the world such as the Angus, Belted Galloway, Charolais, Guernsey, Hereford, Holstein, Jersey, Longhorn and the Simmental. Question, "How long would it take to breed these different cattle together before they turned into chickens?" Answer: NEVER! This "selection process" of breeding cattle can only produce cattle!

And just in case you haven't got it yet...how about **dogs**? There are about 250 different breeds of dogs in the world such as the Akita, Boxer, Dachshund, Greyhound, Mastiff, Pekingese, Saint Bernard, Whippet and the Terrier. So the question is, "How long would it take to breed those different kinds of dogs together before they turned into a dolphin? Answer: NEVER! This "selection process" of breeding dogs can only produce dogs! Therefore, natural selection cannot by nature produce any kind of new creature.[4]

Now folks, I don't know about you, but I'd say based on the problems of the process of natural selection, there's no way it could ever create a new kind of animal, how about you? Therefore, I'd say natural selection is a bunch of bologna, how about you?

Oh, but that's not all. The **second reason** why we know Natural Selection is a lie is because **The Examples Don't Even Work**. People, we're going to take a look at some of the best examples the evolutionists have come up with for supposed proof of natural selection, and you tell me if somebody doesn't have the ol' Pinocchio Syndrome.

Galapagos Finches: During Charles Darwin's five-year voyage on the *H.M.S. Beagle*, he visited the Galapagos Islands in the Pacific. And it was here that he found a group of finches and noticed that there were about 13 varieties of these finches with different sizes and beak types. And even though Darwin never had a day of science training in school, when he saw those variety of finches, he decided that each was a different type of bird showing that his evolution theory had occurred.

However, the only thing this really showed was that variations can and do occur within a created kind. There was no new genetic information added to these finches and no new traits or characteristics had appeared and besides, they were still finches! They never became a spider, chicken, or a weasel!

In fact, one scientist who carefully examined the collection said, 'The whole collection had an appearance of general uniformity. Were it not for the historical importance of these finches as one of the 'pillars' of evidence for evolution, I doubt if much attention would be given them.'

Flies and Bacteria: Some evolutionists point to flies and bacteria that are resistant to DDT and antibiotics as a proof of "evolution in action." However, once again, this is only variation and not the upward changes needed for a new kind of creature altogether and just as in the previous case, no new information was added. Furthermore, when all was said and done, the bacteria remained bacteria and the flies remained flies! They didn't turn into cucumbers, cats or cows!

Peppered Moth: One of the most popular supposed proofs of evolution, especially in the area of natural selection, is the supposed "evolution" of the peppered moth. The peppered moth is a moth species in England that has a light speckled variety and a dark colored variety.

And as the story goes, before 1850, most peppered moths were of the light colored variety but supposedly due to the pollution in the area caused by the Industrial Revolution, the black ones started to become dominant because the black soot from the pollution camouflaged them and so the birds now ate the more visible light colored moths. But when anti-pollution laws began to be enforced years later, the light variety became predominant again because the black ones now lost their camouflage and hence got eaten by the birds again.

The whole idea was brought forth by a man named H.B. Kettlewell and at first his theory and experiments seemed very straightforward. In fact, photographs were taken of the dark and light moths resting on tree trunks during the daytime with birds picking off and eating the less camouflaged ones. In fact, Kettlewell described it as, "The most striking evolutionary change ever actually witnessed in any organism." And British geneticist P.M. Sheppard called it, "The most spectacular evolutionary change ever witnessed and recorded by man." Yes, it was natural selection in action…or was it?

When the supposed evidence was checked out by others, it was actually yet another evolutionary hoax. First of all, after 25 years only two of these moths were seen in their natural habitat. Then it was discovered that peppered moths don't even rest on tree trunks in the daytime like the pictures showed. Rather they are night fliers and hide under leaves in treetops. So to get the desired pictures, Kettlewell and others attracted the moths into traps in the forest with light or by releasing female pheromones.

Then they took dead moths or ones they raised in the laboratory and faked the photographs by pinning or gluing the moths to the trees! In fact, some of the live moths they raised in the lab were so sluggish that they had to warm them up on their car hood to "liven" them up to get the birds to eat them! Furthermore, University of Massachusetts biologist Theodore Sargent who helped glue the moths onto the trees for a NOVA documentary admitted that, "Textbooks and films have featured a lot of fraudulent photographs."

And then evolutionist Jerry Coyne admitted that the peppered moth story, which was "the prize horse in our stable," must now be discarded and said, "My own reaction resembles the dismay attending my discovery, at the age of six, that it was my father and not Santa who brought the presents on Christmas Eve."

And even though the peppered moth story is a complete hoax, many of the writers and textbook publishers still use these same images today all the while knowing it's false. But remember, even it this whole peppered moth story was true, and it's not, it still doesn't prove evolution. Dark moths and light moths have always been around and no matter what color the moth is it's still a moth, not a mouse, a man, or a moose![5]

Now folks, I don't know about you, but I'd say based on the problems with these so-called examples of natural selection, there's no way it could ever create a new kind of animal, how about you? In fact, I'd say it's a bunch of bologna, how about you?

Oh, but that's not all. The **third reason** why we know Natural Selection is a lie is because **The Quotes Don't Even Work**. Now folks, I don't know if you've started to see a pattern over the last several chapters, but how many of you have noticed that every single time the evolutionists admit the mechanisms of evolution don't even work? Well gee, does anybody want to take a guess if the same is true for natural selection? Yes? Wow! You guys are on the ball! But don't take my word for it. Let's listen to theirs.

1. Science Digest, January 1961 said, "Out of 120,000 fertilized eggs of the green frog only two individuals survived. Are we to conclude that these two frogs out of 120,000 were selected by nature because they were the fittest ones? Or rather that natural selection is nothing but blind mortality which selects nothing at all?"

2. G. Simpson, "The Major Features of Evolution," wrote, "It might be argued that the theory of Natural Selection is quite unsubstantiated and has status only as a speculation."

3. Encyclopedia Britannica quoting philosopher Carl Hempel said, "The theory of natural selection is not really an explanation of organic evolution at all—not even a bad one."

4. Tom Bethell, "Darwin's Mistake," Harper Magazine said, "Darwin made a mistake sufficiently serious to undermine his theory. And that mistake has only recently been recognized as such. One organism may indeed be 'fitter' than another but this, of course, is not something which helps create the organism. It is clear, I think, that there was something very, very wrong with such an idea. As I see it the conclusion is pretty staggering: Darwin's theory, I believe, is on the verge of collapse."

5. Niles Eldredge, Curator of Paleontology at the American Museum of Natural History, said, "Natural selection *per se* does not work to create new species."

6. Charles Darwin, The Descent of Man, Vol. 1 said, "I admit that in the earlier editions of my *Origin of Species* I probably attributed too much to the action of natural descent of the survival of the fittest."[6]

Now folks, I don't know about you, but I'd say based on the quotes of the evolutionists themselves, I'd say natural selection is a bunch of bologna, how about you?

Oh but that's still not all. The **fourth reason** why we know Natural Selection is a lie, and a deadly one, is because **The Belief Doesn't Even Work**. People, as we eluded to at the beginning of this chapter, it was Hitler's belief in evolution that gave him the excuse to not only try to conquer the world, but to slaughter millions of people, right? And just in case that's still a hard cookie for some of you to swallow, don't take my word for it, let's listen to the man and people themselves.

What most people don't realize is that the belief of natural selection's survival of the fittest reached its logical conclusion with Adolf Hitler and the Nazi Party. In fact, Hitler himself was not only an evolutionist but even His famous book "Mein Kemp" which means "My Struggle" clearly shows this. The whole theme was about a struggle between races where the Aryan race was charged to dominate and rule the world. For instance, listen to these quotes:

1. R. Milner, Encyclopedia of Evolution said, "During the 1930s, Adolf Hitler believed he was carrying Darwinism forward with his doctrine that undesirable individuals (and inferior races) must be eliminated in the creation of the New Order dominated by Germany's Master Race. German intellectuals believed natural selection was a law of nature impelling them to bloody struggle for domination. Their political and military textbooks promoted Darwin's theories as the 'scientific' basis of a quest for world conquest, with the full backing of German scientists and professors of biology."

2. Robert Clark, Darwin: Before and After said, "One need not read far in Hitler's Mein Kampf to find that evolution likewise influenced him and his views on the master race, genocide, human breeding experiments, etc."

3. R. Milner, Encyclopedia of Evolution said, "The position in Germany was that man must 'conform' to nature's processes, no matter how ruthless. The 'fittest' must never stand in the way of the law of evolutionary progress. In its extreme form, that social view was used in Nazi Germany to justify sterilization and mass murder of the 'unfit,' 'incompetent,' 'inferior races.'"

4. Edward Simon, "Another Side to the Evolution Problem" said, "I cannot deny that the theory of evolution, and the atheism it engendered, led to the moral climate that made a holocaust possible."

5. And Hitler himself said this, "I regard Christianity as the most fatal, seductive lie that has ever existed." "He who would live must fight; he who does not wish to fight, in this world where permanent struggle is the law of life, has not the right to exist." The question we have to ask ourselves is this. "Would Hitler have acted the way he did if he were a creationist?"[7]

Now folks, my whole point in bringing that up is this. It's obvious that what you believe determines how you behave, right? Therefore, a belief in natural selection is not only pretty dumb, it's pretty deadly, how about you? And keep in mind folks, the whole thing is based on a lie!

But you might be thinking, "Okay so maybe the supposed evolution of man and animals is a bunch of bologna and even this thing called natural selection is a bunch of bologna. But what about all the other supposed mechanisms they come up with for evolution? You know, like embryology and mutations and vestigial organs and all that other stuff as to how life supposedly evolved? Well, hey, great question! I guess that's why we'll take a look at that in the next chapter!

Chapter Twenty

The Lie of Embryology

Call it luck or call it fate, but in 1904, an African Pygmy named Ota Benga had just somehow escaped the massacre of his village by a group of thugs working for the Belgium government. Although his wife and children were all murdered and their bodies mutilated, Ota himself was later captured and sold into slavery.

From there he was shipped and displayed in the anthropology wing of the 1904 St. Louis World's Fair as evidence for evolution. It was here that organizers wanted to draw a distinction between the 'darkest Blacks' against the 'dominant whites' showing they were of a 'lower' evolutionary culture.

And if that wasn't bad enough, after the World's fair, Ota found himself at the Bronx Zoo thanks to a Dr. William T. Hornaday. Why? Because he believed there was no apparent difference between a wild beast and the little Black man so he built Ota Benga a new exhibit to live in.

So Ota was given a parrot and an Orangutan named Dohong as cage-mates to keep him company in his captivity and was encouraged to spend as much time as he wanted inside the monkey house. In fact, they even gave him a bow and arrow and told him to shoot it is part of "an exhibit."

But in time Ota Benga began to hate being the object of evolutionary curiosity with nearly every man, woman and child making a beeline for the monkey house to see the wild man from Africa. And here they howled, jeered and yelled at him, but they also poked him in the ribs or tripped him up while everyone laughed at him.

And even though Ota was later allowed to leave the zoo to lead a "normal life," he had a hard time adjusting after his evolutionary experience. So in 1916, after growing homesick and in despair, Ota Benga borrowed a revolver and shot himself in the heart, ending his life.[1]

Now how many of you guys have ever heard the story of Ota Benga before? Yeah, hardly any of us have? Why? Well, I think the answer's pretty obvious. You see, the reason why the man Ota Benga was treated like an ape was because of evolution. And folks, I don't know about you, but I'd say that's just a little bit racist! And gee folks, I guess that's why we need to continue in our study called, "The Witness of Creation." And so far we've seen the first three evidences of creation that God has left behind for us showing us that He's not just real, but that we really can have a personal intimate relationship with Him, the Creator of the universe was the evidences of An Intelligent Creation from very the Hand of Almighty God, as opposed to blind chance exploding from some sort of primeval blob, and then A Young Creation, as opposed to the long-age fairy tale time of evolution. And in the last three chapters we've seen how the third evidence was A Special Creation. And in the last chapter we saw that not only is the supposed ape-man and animal evolution a bunch of bologna, but so is natural selection. Why? Because as we saw, it's got some serious problems. The Process Doesn't Work, the Examples Don't Work, the Quotes Don't Work, and even the Belief Doesn't Work! Therefore, we came to the conclusion that natural selection is not only a lie, it's a deadly one!

But you might be thinking, "Okay, maybe the supposed evolution of people and animals and natural selection is a bunch of bologna, but what about the other supposed mechanisms they come up with, like **embryology**? You know, where we supposedly retrace our common evolutionary history while being embryos?" Well, hey, great question! But before we look at that, let's once again get reacquainted with the Biblical answer for the existence of life.

Isaiah 44:21-24 "Remember these things, O Jacob, for you are my servant, O Israel. I have made you, you are my servant; O Israel, I will not forget you. I have swept away your offenses like a cloud, your sins like the morning mist. Return to me, for I have redeemed you. Sing for joy, O heavens, for the LORD has done this; shout aloud, O earth beneath. Burst into song, you mountains, you forests and all your trees, for the LORD has redeemed Jacob, he displays his glory in Israel. This is what the LORD says – your Redeemer, who formed you in the womb: I am the LORD, who has made all things, who alone stretched out the heavens, who spread out the earth by myself."

Now folks, according to our text, the Bible is clear. Once again, God is not only the One who made the heavens and earth, but what? He's also the One responsible for our birth, right? But once again, what does evolution teach? Do they say that God's the One Who made us and even knew us while still in the womb? Are you kidding! They say it was purely by chance in an embryonic goo, right? Therefore, I'd say we better take a look at not just the Scriptural evidence but the scientific evidence of this supposed **embryology** thing and see who's telling the truth, how about you? But before we do that, let's first take a refresher course in how this embryology thing is supposed to work.

The idea of embryology or "ontogeny recapitulates phylogeny" began with Evolutionist and German zoologist Ernst Haeckel in his 1876 book *General Morphology of Organisms*. According to this view, as a fertilized egg develops to form an embryo, it actually repeats its evolutionary history. And as evidence, Haeckel examined and drew pictures of the embryos of a fish, frog, chicken, pig and human and said there was a remarkable similarity among them in their stages of development. Therefore, it was believed that by observing these embryonic similarities, it would be like watching a "silent moving picture" of our evolutionary past.

And what's interesting is that even though Haeckel says he started out being a Christian, it was admittedly after reading Charles Darwin's *Origin of the Species* in 1860 that he "converted" into an evolutionist. So with an almost religious zealousness, he was determined to find evidence for evolution to the point where he came up with his theory and was actually called "Darwin's Bulldog." So to help propagate his new "religion," Haeckel drew enormous backdrops showing pictures of his embryos and toured from city to city giving his presentation to the point where it was called a sort of 'Darwinian passion play'!

In fact, Darwin believed that Haeckel's enthusiasm was the main reason for the success of evolution being accepted in Germany. Then Haeckel also came up with a new missing link, which he called *Pithecanthropus alalus or* "speechless apeman" and even had an artist draw the imagined creature and his supposed wife. And later a Dutch scientist concluded that since neither one of them could speak, "It must have been a happy marriage because his wife could not contradict him."

And so much so was Haeckel's idea of evolutionary embryology popularized that even today we see it's influence behind things such as Freudian psychology where Freud believed that in order to understand dysfunctional behavior today, we need understand our earlier stages of evolutionary development.

Also, Dr. Spock, the popular child development specialist said, "Each child as he develops is retracing the whole history of mankind, physically and spiritually, step by step. A baby starts off in the womb as a single tiny cell, just the way the first living thing appeared in the ocean. Weeks later, as he lies in the amniotic fluid of the womb, he has gills like a fish."[2]

And then just in case there's any doubt, as recent as 1986, the *Reader's Digest Book of Facts* stated that Haeckel's theory is an established fact.[2]

Now folks, how many of you ever heard about or were taught this embryology theory before? Well, most of us have, especially in Biology class, right? But the point is this. Is it really true? Do we actually retrace our evolutionary history while still in the embryonic stage? Absolutely not! In fact, it's another big fat lie! How do I know?

Because the **first reason** why we know Embryology is a lie is because **There's Problems with the Theory**. People, we're going to take a look at some very serious problems with this embryology thing and you tell me if we haven't been lied to, yet again!

The "Chicken Sac" Problem: Haeckel said that the similarity of the chicken or "egg yolk sac" in his diagram of various embryos was proof that they are all retracing their so-called similar evolutionary past. However, in a baby chick, the yolk sac is its source of nourishment until it hatches. This is because the chick is in a shell, without a connection to its mother. But we, on the other hand, grow attached to our mothers, and they nourish us.

As it turns out, in a human, the so-called "egg yolk pouch" serves a totally different purpose. It's actually a pouch that produces blood for the infant. You see, our blood is made in our bones; but, when we were an embryo, we had no bones! So God gave us a tiny sac-like organ to make our blood for us, otherwise we'd die. That's what our embryonic sac is for. The only similarity of this bulging sac is its shape! It's not a throwback to an earlier "chicken stage" and therefore it has nothing to do with supposed "similar" evolutionary beginnings.

The Tail Problem: Then Haeckel said that the similarity of the "tail structure" in his embryo drawings was proof that they are all retracing their so-called similar evolutionary past. Now yes, animals do go on to develop a tail but the part that was identified as a "tail" in humans by Haeckel and his followers is in fact the backbone, which "resembles" a tail only because it takes shape before the legs do.

When we were an embryo, our spines were longer than our bodies. Therefore, it stuck out and looked like a so-called "tail" but it has nothing to do with a tail! It's because our spine is very complicated and initially required extra space to develop. Therefore, these so-called "tail structures" are not a throwback to an "animal stage" and it has nothing to do with supposed "similar" evolutionary beginnings.

The Gill Slit Problem: Haeckel also said that the similarity of the gill slits or "fish gills" in his embryo drawings was proof that they are all retracing their so-called similar evolutionary past. Now yes, in a fish, these gill slits do develop into fully functional gills by which the fish breathe by extracting oxygen out of the water. However, in humans, it is now known that these so-called "gill slits" or "openings" are not openings at all nor do they extract oxygen out of the water.

Instead, scientists now know that the these "folds" the upper one, eventually develops into the middle ear canals, then the middle fold changes into the parathyroids, and the bottom fold becomes the thymus gland. As one guy put it, "They are little folds of skin in humans that have nothing to do with breathing. I've seen fat people with five or six chins and they can't breath though any of them but the top one. Therefore, these "gill slits" are not a throwback to a "fish stage" and it has nothing to do with supposed "similar" evolutionary beginnings.

The Retracing Problem: And then finally, there's the whole premise of this "retracing" of our supposed "similar" evolutionary beginnings. Sure enough, we start as small, round structures looking somewhat like single cells. But notice how superficial that argument is. If we were to just look at outward appearances of "small round structures" then could we not say that we're also related to a marble or a ball bearing? They're small and they're round!

But even an evolutionist would respond that this is crazy. But that's exactly the point. If you take a look on the inside, not just the outside, the "small round dot" we each start form is totally different from the first cell of every other kind of life. Now yes, a mouse, an elephant, and a human are identical in size and shape outwardly at the moment of conception.

But in terms of DNA and proteins, inwardly, right at conception, each of these types of life is as totally different chemically as they will ever be structurally. In fact, even if we wanted to or even by mistake a human still cannot produce a yolk or gills or a tail, because we just don't have, and never had, those same DNA instructions. Therefore, the whole premise of "retracing" our so-called evolutionary beginnings based on similar "outward" structures is bogus.[3]

Now folks, I don't know about you, but I'd say based on the problems with the theory of embryology, I'd say there's no stinkin' way it could ever provide evidence for evolution, how about you? And therefore, that would make embryology a what? A lie! Hmmm, What a shocker!

Oh, but that's not all. The **second reason** why we know Embryology is a lie is because **There's Problems with the Evidence**. People, we're going to take a look at the supposed evidence for this embryology thing, and you tell me if somebody doesn't need to be sent to the corner for lying!

The Picture Problem: The only problem with all those pictures and diagrams of embryos that Haeckel used to almost single handedly convert Germany to evolution was they were yet another evolutionary hoax! Since Haeckel was an accomplished artist, as well as an anatomist, he used his art talent to alter the real drawings of various animals to make them look more alike so that it "appeared" as if embryonic recapitulation were true.

In fact, his drawings were so bad and inaccurate that they were exposed as frauds in 1874 as well as his data shown to be completely manufactured. In its September 5, 1997, issue, the famous journal *Science* published an article revealing that Haeckel's embryo drawings had been falsified. The article described how the embryos were in fact very different from one another.

Observations in recent years have revealed that embryos of different species do not resemble each other, as Haeckel had attempted to show. The great differences between the mammal, reptile and bat embryos are a clear instance of this. It is clear they are not only severely different, but Haeckel severely altered them. In fact, it is now known that in order to get the "desired" results, Haeckel deliberately removed some organs and added some imaginary ones.

The Conviction Problem: Not only were Haeckel's drawings exposed as obvious frauds in 1874, but he was even convicted of his fraud by his own university. At Jena, the university where he taught, Haeckel was charged with fraud by five professors and convicted by a university court.

His deceit was exposed in a book called "Haeckel's Frauds and Forgeries," released in 1915. And quoting 19 leading authorities of the day, they said, "It was a fraud from the beginning. Haeckel fraudulently presented altered, misleading and misinterpreted evidence. Some of the key details of his embryo drawings were purposely altered to make a case for Evolution where none existed."

And as a result of being found guilty and convicted, disrepute followed Haeckel for the remainder of his professional career.) However, even after all this fraudulent behavior, Haeckel still blamed others for his behavior saying, "Other evolutionists had committed similar offences." But even though it was proven that Haeckel's drawings were falsified, the whole world of science continued to be deceived by them for over a century.

The Fraud Problem: Believe it or not, in spite of the fact that Haeckel's drawings were proven completely fake back in 1874, they are still in most Biology textbooks today! For instance, fraudulent pictures are still being used to support Haeckels' theory in a textbook called Biology Sixth Edition as recent as 2004 by Raven and Johnson.

Now either the authors are ignorant of the truth or they're deliberately lying to promote their religion of evolution. In fact, embryologist Michael Richardson said in Science Magazine: "Sadly, it is the discredited 1874 drawings that are used in so many British and American biology textbooks."[4]

Now folks, I don't know about you, but I'd say based on the supposed evidence of embryology, if that's the best you can come up with, I'd say somebody's theory's in trouble, how about you? But not only that, I'd say embryology is a what? A lie! Hmmm, shocker!

Oh, but that's not all. The **third reason** why we know Embryology is a lie is because **There's Problems with the Quotes**. People, I don't know if you're thinking what I'm thinking but gee whiz man, I mean you'd think if there was such obvious problems with this theory that even the evolutionist's would have to admit it, right? Well, guess what? You're right! Let's listen to what the evolutionists have to say about embryology, and you tell me if even they know it's a bunch of bologna.

1. Dr. Stephen J. Gould admitted that: "Haeckel had exaggerated the similarities [between embryos of different species] by idealizations and omissions. He also, in some cases — in a procedure that can only be called fraudulent — simply copied the same figure over and over again. Haeckel's drawings never fooled expert embryologists, who recognized his fudgings right from the start. Haeckel's drawings, despite their noted inaccuracies, entered into the most impenetrable and permanent of all quasi-scientific literatures: standard student textbooks of biology.

   Once ensconced in textbooks, misinformation becomes cocooned and effectively permanent, because…textbooks copy from previous texts. We do, I think, have the right to be both astonished and ashamed by the century of mindless recycling that has led to the persistence of these drawings in a large number, if not a majority of modern textbooks!"

2. Anatomist F. Keibel of Freiburg University "It clearly appears that Haeckel has in many cases freely invented embryos, or reproduced the illustrations given by others in a substantially changed form."

3. Zoologist L. Rütimeyer of Basle University called his distorted drawings. "A sin against scientific truthfulness."

4. Dr. Michael Richardson an embryologist at St. George's Medical School in London said, "This is one of the worst cases of scientific fraud. It's shocking to find that somebody one thought was a great scientist was deliberately misleading. It makes me angry. What Haeckel did was to take a human embryo and copy it, pretending that the salamander and the pig and all the others looked the same at the same stage of development. They don't. These are fakes."

5. Embryologist Erich Blechschmidt said that Haeckel's theory was "One of the most serious errors in the history of biology. The so-called basic law of biogenetics is wrong. No buts or ifs can mitigate this fact. It is not even a tiny bit correct or correct in a different form. It is totally wrong."

6. Sir Arthur Keith stated: "Now that the appearance of the embryo at all stages is known, the general feeling is one of disappointment; the human embryo at no stage is anthropoid in appearance. The embryo of the mammal never resembles the worm, the fish, or the reptile. Embryology provides no support whatsoever for the evolutionary hypothesis."

7. In their classic biology textbook, *Life: An Introduction to Biology*, George Gaylord Simpson and William S. Beck put it bluntly when they wrote: "You may well ask why we bother you with the principles that turned out to be wrong. There are two reasons. In the first place, belief in recapitulation became so widespread that it is still evident in some writings about biology and evolution. You should know therefore what recapitulation is supposed to be, and you should know that it does not really occur. It is now firmly established that ontogeny does not recapitulate phylogeny."[5]

Now folks, I don't know about you, but I'd say based on the quotes of the evolutionists themselves, even they know that embryology is a bunch of bologna, how about you? But not only that, even they know it's a what? A lie! Hmmm, shocker!

Oh, but that's still not all. The **fourth reason** why we know Embryology is a lie is because **There's Problems with the Belief**. People, as we saw at the beginning of this chapter, it was the belief in evolution that provided the justification for the rotten racial treatment of Ota Benga, right? Well folks, believe it or not, that's the tip of the iceberg! Not only is the lie of embryology still being used in textbooks today, but it's still being used to justify abortion with such mind-boggling statements as appears below.

Amazingly, one can still occasionally find Haeckel's theory of "embryonic recapitulation" being taught or implied in schools and universities. Some "pro-choice" advocates and abortion clinics have even used this evolutionary concept to make abortion more palatable: "We're not cutting up a baby; it's just a fish or a jellyfish. It's not human; it's just tissue." Once again, deceptive evolutionary claims produce tragic results.

As an example, consider the case of the late evolutionist, Carl Sagan. He and his wife wrote and argued for the need for abortion saying that, "The human embryo first is "a kind of parasite" that eventually looks like a "segmented worm." Also it is revealed that they have "gill arches" like that of a "fish or amphibian" and "reptilian" features that later give rise to "mammalian pig-like" traits" Thus by the end of the second month, according to these two authors, the creature resembles a "primate but is still not quite human."[6]

And people, to show you how deadly this evolutionary lie has become, let's take a look at the results of today's modern day holocaust called abortion.

1. 48% of pregnancies among American women are unintended and ½ of these are killed by abortion.

2. Each year, 2 out of every 100 women from age 15-44 have an abortion and 47% of them have had at least one previous abortion.

3. An estimated 43% of women will have at least 1 abortion by the time they are 45 years old.

4. During the Revolutionary War 25,000 Americans died. During the Civil War nearly 500,000 people died. During WWI over 100,000 people died. During WWII about 400,000 Americans died. And both the Korean and Vietnam wars added up to about 113,000 being killed. However, since 1973 in the war on the unborn, we have had 50,000,000 babies murdered by abortion in America. As one man said, "And we pray, 'Oh God bless America.' God says, 'Forget it. I'm getting ready to judge you folks!'"

5. And believe it or not, each year an estimated 46 million abortions occur worldwide. I'd say God's about to judge the world as well![7]

Now folks, I don't know about you, but we can pray all day long for God to Bless America, but unless we stop this slaughter of innocent children, I'd say God really is going to judge America, how about you? And keep in mind folks, the whole time it's all based on an evolutionary lie!

But you might be thinking, "Okay so maybe the supposed evolution of man and animals and natural selection and embryology are a bunch of bologna. But what about all the other supposed mechanisms they come up with? You know, like mutations and vestigial organs and transitional fossils and punctuated equilibrium and all that other stuff as to how life supposedly evolved? Well, hey, great question! I guess that's why we'll take a look at in the next chapter!

Chapter Twenty-One

The Lie of Mutations and Vestigial Organs

It's been called one of the biggest exterminations in modern history and it was spawned by a belief in evolution.

It happened to the Aboriginal people in the land down under. In 1870, an evolutionary anthropologist named Max Muller had divided the human race into seven categories. And it just so happened that the Aborigines fell at the bottom.

And so as a result of this racist, ruthless, and savage view, a terrible massacre began with the goal of exterminating them. Aboriginal heads were nailed over station doors. Poisoned bread was given to their families. And in many parts of Australia, aboriginal settlements completely disappeared within just 50 years.

But believe it or not, they weren't just killed because they were thought to be an inferior race, they were killed to help support the theory of evolution.

Not only were the local police, but even the locals were given instructions on how to rob their graves and plug up bullet wounds in freshly killed "specimens".

In fact, a New South Wales missionary was horrified to witness a slaughter by mounted police of dozens of Aboriginal men, women and children. Forty-five heads were then boiled down and the 10 best skulls were packed off for overseas for display.

In fact, Charles Darwin himself wrote and asked for Tasmanian skulls when only four of the island's Aborigines were left alive, provided his request would not 'upset' their feelings.

And believe it or not, the demand has not entirely stopped. Aboriginal bones have still been sought by major institutions as evidence for evolution. In fact, the Smithsonian Institute in Washington D.C. still has thousands of them on hand.[1]

Now folks, how many of you guys ever heard of the slaughter of the Aborigines before? Yeah, hardly any of us. And gee whiz, I wonder why? Could it be that the reason why the Aboriginal people were treated like animals was because of evolution? Uh huh. No wonder you never hear about that, right? And therefore, at this rate, we don't need to call it evolution, we need to call it evilution! Hello! It's not just racist, it's deadly! And people, that's exactly why we're going to continue in our study called, "The Witness of Creation." And so far we've seen the first three evidences of creation that God has left behind for us showing us that He's not just real, but that we really can have a personal intimate relationship with Him, the Creator of the universe was the evidences of An Intelligent Creation from very the Hand of Almighty God, as opposed to blind chance exploding from some sort of primeval blob, and then A Young Creation, as opposed to the long-age fairy tale time of evolution. And in the last four chapters we've saw how the third evidence was A Special Creation. And there we've not only seen how the supposed evolution of people and animals and natural selection is a bunch of bologna, but in the last chapter we saw that embryology was also a bunch a bologna. Why? Because as we saw, it's got some serious problems. It's got Problems with the Theory, Problems with the Evidence, Problems with the Quotes, and Problems with the Belief! It's actually the justification people use for abortion! And therefore, we came to the conclusion that embryology is not only a lie, it's a deadly one!

But you might be thinking, "Okay so maybe the supposed evolution of people and animals and natural selection and embryology is a bunch of bologna. But what about the other supposed mechanisms they've come up with, like **mutations** and **vestigial organs**? Well, hey, great question! But before we look at that, let's once again get reacquainted with the Biblical answer for the existence of life.

Jeremiah 27:1-6 "Early in the reign of Zedekiah son of Josiah king of Judah, this word came to Jeremiah from the LORD: This is what the LORD said to me: Make a yoke out of straps and crossbars and put it on your neck. Then send word to the kings of Edom, Moab, Ammon, Tyre and Sidon through the envoys who have come to Jerusalem to Zedekiah king of Judah. Give them a message for their masters and say, This is what the LORD Almighty, the God of Israel, says: Tell this to your masters: With my great power and outstretched arm I made the earth and its people and the animals that are on it, and I give it to anyone I please. Now I will hand all your countries over to my servant Nebuchadnezzar king of Babylon; I will make even the wild animals subject to him."

Now folks, according to our text, the Bible is clear. Once again, God and God alone had the power to do what? To create all of life, right? From the heavens to the humans, right? But once again, what does evolution teach? Do they say that God's the One Who stretched out His arm and brought us into being? Are you kidding! They say it was a bunch of luck in some primordial sea, right? Therefore, I'd say we better take a look at not just the Scriptural evidence but the scientific evidence of these supposed evolutionary mechanisms of mutations and vestigial organs and see who's telling the truth, how about you? And to help us do that, let's first take a look at **mutations**. Here's how the basic premise goes.

Evolutionists believe that over millions and billions of years, that there has been millions and billions of what they call beneficial mutations that have given rise to all the species we see today. For instance, they say an early fish might have accidentally grown a new beneficial kind of fin that helped it swim faster and escape his enemies. Or maybe its fins mutated into legs and it was able to walk on land.

And folks, unless you think I'm making this up, listen to this. Carl Sagan said:

"The evolution of life on Earth is a product of random events, chance mutations, and individually unlikely steps." And evolutionary scientist Theodosius Dobzhansky said, "The process of mutations is the only known source of the new materials of genetic variability, and hence of evolution."[2]

So my question is this? Is this really true? Are millions and billions of mutations over millions and billions of years what really brought life into being? Are you kidding? People, it's another evolutionary lie! How do I know?

Because the **first reason** why we know evolution by way of **mutations** is a lie is because **There's Problems with the Theory**! People, we're going to take a look at some serious problems with this supposed evolution by way of mutations and you tell me if we haven't been lied to.

The Problem of Rarity: The only problem with mutations causing all of life to come into being is because in the first place they are extremely rare. In fact, they almost never occur. For instance, even the *World Book Encyclopedia* said that "Most genes mutate only once in 100,000 generations or more. Researchers estimate that a human gene may remain stable for 2 ½ million years."

First of all, as we've seen earlier, we have A Young Creation of only a few thousand years and since we haven't been around for 2 ½ million years, there hasn't been enough time for mutations to work.

But secondly, even if we ignore this and follow the evolutionist's timescale, this extremely rare occurrence of mutations dooms the possibility of ever producing the vast amount of various plant and animal species with millions and millions of characteristics found all over the world. There isn't enough time for mutations to work!

The Problem of Damage: As we saw earlier, the evolutionists believe that not only mutations have caused evolution to take place but that these mutations were "beneficial." However, nothing could be further from the truth! It is now known that mutations don't help an organism, they damage, mutilate, or kill the organism!

For instance, the evolutionists thought they had a major breakthrough in 1928, when X rays were discovered which would allow the to "speed up" mutations. Whereas, in nature, there might be one mutation, now they could not only instantly manufacture millions of them but also focus them on just one organism!

They thought for sure they were going to be able to create a whole new species right before their very eyes. The results? Mutations are found not to be beneficial but detrimental. They harmed, damaged, and weakened the organism so bad that most of them died and those that didn't die, their offspring had a tendency to die shortly thereafter!

Therefore, because of the damaging affects of mutations, they could never make life evolve into something better but rather they ensure that death would come to everyone. Just the opposite of evolution!

In fact, one person actually has a deformed foot with more toes than normal, eight to be exact. Is this beneficial? Well, other than having a hard time finding a pair of socks, he can't run any faster. In fact, it probably inhibits his ability to run as well as others and so guess who gets eaten by the lion first? That's right! Johnny No Socks!

Or there's all kinds of deformed frogs out there missing legs. Is this beneficial? Well, he certainly can't hop better and a one-legged frog has a tendency to hop in circles! Now even though that's a cool trick, guess who the bird's going to eat first?

Or some sheep have actually mutated where one has extremely short and stubby legs. Is he better off? Are you kidding? He's easy prey! When the wolf comes his friends can yell all they want "Run Sparky run!" but in the end they'll say, "Oops! Too bad you had short legs Sparky. Nice knowing you!

Therefore, since mutations are found not to be beneficial but detrimental, there's no way they could ever cause evolution to happen!

The Problem of Logic: Evolutionists believe that a purely random mutation or "accident" in a creature is somehow going to make that creature better. However, let's apply this logic of "random accidents" elsewhere in life.

For instance, if **poked a stick** into somebody's bike spokes as they were riding by, would it make their bike ride more enjoyable? No! They'd become road pizza right?

Or if you spontaneously decided to **rewire the inside of the TV** set at a Superbowl party, would you be the hit of the game? No! They'd make a game out of hitting you, right?

Or how many of you when you got into an **unexpected car wreck** discovered that afterwards, your car worked even better than before? No! You found out that your insurance bill went up higher than before right?

Or how about the nuclear accident that occurred at **Chernobyl**? Surely this should have been an evolutionary paradise with all that radiation mutating everything, right? Are you kidding! Rather than creating new life, it utterly destroyed life.

For instance, after the Chernobyl accident it caused 800,000 children to see instant medical treatment, the price of the cleanup and the value of lost farmland and production cost $358 billion dollars, each passing year brings more and more birth defects among farm animals, colts with eight limbs, animals with deformed lower jaws, and disjointed spinal columns, no eyes, deformed skulls, and distorted mouths, stillbirths, and infant deaths among the animals.

What about the people? There has begun a dramatic rise in thyroid disease, anemia, cancer, and an astounding drop in the immunity level of the entire population. And through it all no new species have come into existence; only the same ones that have always been there who are now damaged and dying. In fact, the latest death toll caused by Chernobyl is now up to 10,000 people.

Or how about the **Atomic Bomb**? Surely lots of fine new species should have been produced here. Maybe Chernobyl wasn't big enough for mutation. Well, when the atomic bomb of Hiroshima was dropped, it set off a blast with the force of 13,000 tons of TNT and destroyed more than 4.5 square miles of the city, with over 92,000 persons dead or missing.

And what of the living who had radiation poured all over their bodies? They were worse off than the dead. They struggled with radiation-damaged bodies through the remainder of their shortened lives and not one of them evolved into a different species or a new super-race.

Therefore, since mutations don't help an organism, but damage, mutilate, or kill an organism, there's no way it could cause evolution to take place! And I guess that why geneticist C.H. Waddington said in *Science Today*, "This is really the theory that… strikes me as a lunatic sort of logic, and I think we should be able to do better."[3]

Oh, but that's not all. The **second reason** why we know evolution by way of **mutations** is a lie is because **There's Problems with the Examples!** **Example of the Fruit Fly:** One of the most popular examples of supposed beneficial mutations is the decades of research done on fruit flies. It seemed like an ideal candidate. First of all, they breed very rapidly and require little food and each of its offspring matures in a only a few days.

Therefore, the evolutionists believed that what it would take mammals tens of thousands of years to accomplish, the humble fruit flies could do within a very short amount of time. In fact, the experiments done on fruit flies have already exceeded the equivalent of a supposed million years of people living on earth.

So they went right to work and after decades of study, outside of those that were immediately killed or sterilized, 400 different mutational features were identified in fruit flies. Some had more wings or less wings or more eyes or less eyes or more legs or less legs. And when all was said and done…the fruit fly always remained a fruit fly!

After 80 years and millions of generations of fruit flies subjected to X rays and chemicals which cause mutations, all they have been able to produce are more of the same: fruit flies. In fact, the survivors also had a tendency to revert over succeeding generations back to the original form! Researchers discovered that it was as if some kind of genetic repair mechanism took over and blocked any possibility of evolution.

As one guy said, "God was very careful in Genesis to state that each of the animals were created 'after his kind.' After 80 years and millions of generations, God was proven right: A fruit fly will always be a fruit fly."

Example of Bacteria: Evolutionists are quick to say that certain bacteria have become resistant to certain drugs and that these "resistant strains" of bacteria are the result of mutations showing evolution in action. However, all that was discovered was that bacteria like other forms of life can have variations.

First of all, some of those bacteria could resist the drugs while others could not. Some of the bacteria survived and some did not. All that the physicians were doing by administering drugs was to breed new, stronger strains of bacteria! Mutations had nothing to do with the process!

Secondly, the transfer of resistance genes was already existent in the bacteria and the building of resistance came as a result of losing genetic data not gaining it. And thirdly, when all was said and done, bacteria stayed bacteria! That's not evolution!

Example of Disease: Believe it or not, evolutionists say that the disease called Sickle Cell Anemia is proof of a "beneficial" mutation. This is because, it has been discovered that a person who has Sickle Cell Anemia is less likely to contract malaria from mosquitoes! But is this really a true benefit?

As one guy said, "That's like getting your leg chopped off so you can't get athlete's foot!" Or that like saying if you had polio your less likely to be killed in an auto accident because your paralyzed and stuck in a bed."

Furthermore, it has been shown that cystic fibrosis and even cancer are a result of a kind of mutated gene. Question, "How many of you would volunteer to acquire these diseases so you can live a more 'beneficial' life?"

Sin is the Reason: "What conclusions may be drawn from these few examples, and countless others like them? First, that the human mutation problem is bad and getting worse. Second, that it is unbalanced by any detectable positive mutations. This research affirms the reality of the past Biblical curse of decay and degeneration on the world of nature, as stated in both the Old and New Testaments.

It also highlights the grim reality of the future hopelessness of the human race without the saving intervention of God and His Christ. Mutations continue to slowly harm us. Each generation has a slightly more disordered genetic constitution than the preceding one, and no amount of eugenics can reverse this process of decay. Gene therapy may mask the effects, but it will not reverse the underlying degenerative process.

How ironic it is that the byproduct of the fall of man, sin, which is why we have suffering and disease, is now touted by the evolutionists as a good thing."[4]

Oh, but that's still not all. The **third reason** why we know evolution by way of **mutations** is a lie is because **There's Problems with the Quotes!**

1. George Gaylord Simpson in "Uniformitarianism: An Inquiry into Principle Theory and Method in Geohistory and Biochemistry," said: "Most mutations with large effects are lethal at an early stage for the individual in which they occur and hence have zero probability of spreading."

2. Herbert Nilsson, in"Synthetic Speciation" said: 'There is no single instance where it can be maintained that any of the mutants studied has a higher vitality than the mother species. It is, therefore, absolutely impossible to build a current evolution on mutations."

3. Pierre-Paul de Grasse, "Evolution of Living Organisms" said: "No matter how numerous they may be, mutations do not produce any kind of evolution."

4. Julian Huxley, "Major Features of Evolution" said: "Obviously, such a process [species change through mutations] has played no part whatever in evolution."[5]

Now folks, I don't know about you, but I'd say based on the problems, examples, and quotes we just saw, I'd say somebody's mutated something all right, they've "mutated a few of the facts," you now what I'm saying? And gee, that would make this evolution by way of mutations a what? Another big fat lie! Hmmm. Shocker!

Oh, but that's not all. As if the lie of mutations wasn't big enough, there's yet another one out there that evolutionist's say is genuine proof of evolution in action. It's called **vestigial organs**. How many of you ever heard those? Yeah, it's pretty commonplace. And the basic premise goes like this. Darwin believed that since there seemed to be various organs in animals that were "vestigial" or "unused" that this was proof of evolution. And it's believed that these "unused" organs in people are actually the left over remnants of our non-human ancestors. And for proof, they even compiled a list of almost 200 of these supposed "unused" or vestigial organs. In fact, as recent as 1997, *Encyclopedia Britannica* said:

"The appendix does not serve any useful purpose as a digestive organ in humans, and it is believed to be gradually disappearing in the human species over evolutionary time."[6]

And so here's my question. Is this really true? Are vestigial organs really the left over remnants of our evolution from animals to people? I don't think so! Why? Because it's yet another evolutionary lie! How do I know?

Because the **first reason** why we know evolution by way of **vestigial organs** is a lie is because **There's Problems with the Theory**! People, we're going to take a look at some serious problems with this supposed evolution by way of vestigial organs and you tell me if somebody hasn't spent too much time staring at monkeys!

The Useless Problem: The whole theory of vestigial organs assumes that because something "appears" to be useless then it is no longer needed. However, think about this logic. You could live without both of your legs and both of your arms but that doesn't mean you don't need them. Therefore, a supposed useless organ doesn't mean its not needed. The only thing that's vestigial or useless is this theory!

The Ancestor Problem: One of the most common cited examples of a supposed vestigial organ is the appendix. But as it turns out, humans are not the only one who has an appendix. So do wombats, rabbits, and opossums. Now the evolutionary theory of vestiges is based on the concept that your vestigial organs are inherited from a long line of creatures. So does this mean we evolved from rabbits?

And by the way, as it turns out monkeys don't have an appendix. So how could we have evolved from them like the evolutionists say? Based on their reasoning, since we have an appendix and monkeys don't then they must be a higher evolved creature than us and or have evolved from us, which is just the opposite of what they say!

The Degeneration Problem: The premise of evolution is that we are evolving into better and stronger creatures over time. However, if you stop and think about it, vestiges or useless organs actually proves degeneration instead of evolution! Useless organs in our bodies would mean we were going backwards, not forward. Once again this is directly opposite to what they say!

The Complexity Problem: Another point that needs to be considered is this: If man does have nearly 200 vestigial organs (organs that once were functioning), then in the past he would have had more organs than he now has. That means, the farther back we go in time, the more complex the organism becomes. Once again, this is directly opposite to the evolutionary theory![7]

Oh, but that's not all. The **second reason** why we know evolution by way of **vestigial organs** is a lie is because **There's Problems with the Examples**!

The Appendix: Textbooks often say that there are vestigial organs and again, one of the most common cited examples is the appendix. In fact, evolutionists have suggested it was once part of our herbivore ancestors. But is this organ in our body really useless? Absolutely not!

As it turns out, the appendix is a part of our lymphatic system and therefore affects our immune system and helps fight against infections. Also, the appendix may also boost antibody production in the spleen, and may even play a role in preventing cancer! You can take it out and still live but that doesn't mean it's useless or that it's not needed.

The Fold in the Eye: Charles Darwin said the semi-lunar fold in your eye was useless. However, it's now known it's needed to cleanse and lubricate your eyeball. (Maybe this is what kept him from reading the Bible…he had a crusty eyeball.)

The Tonsils: Tonsils are also cited as a popular so-called useless organ. However, it is now known that our tonsils serve a valuable purpose. They actually have a significant role in protecting the throat against infections, particularly until adolescence. So much for being useless!

The Glands: Believe it or not, various glands in the body are or were once considered absolutely useless by evolutionists, like the thymus, pineal, and thyroid, and pituitary glands. However, we know now that the thymus gland enables the T cells to function properly, which protect your body from infection. The pineal gland secretes important hormones, such as *melatonin*, for proper brain functioning.

The thyroid gland is essential to normal body growth and affects our metabolism and body activity. And finally, the pituitary gland acts as a "master gland," controlling skeletal growth, proper functioning of the thyroid, adrenals, and reproductive glands. (How many of you would still like to have a doctor who believes in vestigial organs?)

The Wisdom Teeth: Some people experience problems with their wisdom teeth and they have to be removed. Well, evolutionists say it's because we no longer need them and they are proof of a vestigial organ. But actually, many people still have healthy, useful wisdom teeth. (I've got all mine…maybe that's why I talk so fast!)

Besides, all this shows is that wisdom teeth represent a physical weakness, like failing eyesight, or hardening of the arteries. This does not suggest poor design or uselessness, but a fallen state from perfect creation.

The Tailbone: The tailbone or coccyx is yet another popular supposed vestigial organ. However, it is vitally important. It's at the bottom of our spine and without it you could not only not sit down comfortably, but it also provides an attachment for your pelvic organs, so they will not collapse. It also serves as an anchor for muscles and tendons and plays a role in giving birth, leg movement, and other functions in the lower torso.

As one guy said, 'Once I was doing a debate in Huntsville, AL. I was debating the president of the North Alabama Atheist Association. And he got up in front of God and everybody and said, 'Folks, we've got proof for evolution. The humans have a tailbone they no longer need.' When it was my turn I got up and I said, 'Mr. Patterson, I taught Biology and Anatomy. I happen to know there are nine little muscles that attach to the tailbone without which you cannot perform some very valuable functions. I will not tell you what they all are, but trust me, you need those muscles.' However Mr. Patterson, if you think the tailbone is vestigial, I will pay to have yours removed. Bend over.' Therefore, it's painfully obvious there are no so-called useless organs in our body![8]

Oh, but that's still not all. The **third reason** why we know evolution by way of **vestigial organs** is a lie is because **There's Problems with the Quotes!**

1. William Straus, "Quarterly Review of Biology" (1947) said: "There is no longer any justification for regarding the appendix as a vestigial structure."

2. P. Erlich and R. Holm, "The Process of Evolution" (1963) "It's shortcomings have been almost universally pointed out by modern authors, but the idea still has a prominent place in biological mythology."

3. S. Scadding, "Evolutionary Theory" (1981) "As our knowledge has increased, the list of vestigial structures has decreased. Even the current short list of vestigial structures in humans is questionable. Since it is not possible to unambiguously identify useless structures, and since the structure of the argument used is not scientifically valid, I conclude that 'vestigial organs' provide no special evidence for the theory of evolution."

4. Dr. R.L. Wysong noted: "Not too long ago man was imputed to have 180 vestiges. Organs like the appendix, tonsils, thymus, pineal gland and thyroid gland were on the list. Today, all former vestigial organs are known to have some function during the life of the individual.

If the organ has any function at any time, it cannot be called rudimentary or vestigial. As man's knowledge has increased the list of vestigial organs decreased. So what really was vestigial? Was it not man's rudimentary knowledge of the intricacies of the body?"[9]

Now folks, I don't know about you, but I'd say based on the problems, examples, and quotes we just saw of vestigial organs, I'd say somebody's got a vestige all right, they've got a "vestigial brain cell or two" you know what I'm saying? And gee, that would make this evolution by way of vestigial organs a what? Another big fat lie! Hmmm. Shocker! In fact, I'd say based on this kind of track record, any kind of evolutionary mechanism they come up is probably also going to be a lie, how about you?

But you might be thinking, "Okay so maybe the supposed evolution of man and animals is a bunch of bologna and even the supposed mechanisms of natural selection, embryology, mutations and vestigial organs are a bunch of bologna. But what the remaining mechanisms they've come up with for evolution? You know, like transitional fossils, punctuated equilibrium, sequential ordering and all that other stuff as to how life supposedly evolved? Well, hey, great question! I guess that's why we'll take a look at in the next chapter!

Chapter Twenty-Two

The Lie of Fossil Transitions

Dr. Eric Pianka gave a speech to the Texas Academy of Science last month in which he advocated the need to exterminate 90% of the population through the airborne ebola virus.

Standing in front of a slide of human skulls, Pianka gleefully advocated this virus as his preferred method of extermination, choosing it over AIDS because of its faster kill period.

Ebola victims suffer the most tortuous deaths imaginable as the virus kills by liquefying the internal organs. The body literally dissolves as the victim writhes in pain bleeding from every orifice.

Pianka also suggests that we should begin to sterilize the human population now saying that, 'We need to sterilize everybody on the earth and make the antidote freely available to anyone willing to work for it.'

And believe it or not, not only was Pianka later presented with a distinguished scientist award by the Academy, but amazingly the audience of fellow scientists and students actually applauded, cheered, and laughed approvingly.

And Pianka is no crackpot. He has given lectures to prestigious universities worldwide where he is merely echoing the elites hideous interest in depopulation techniques via Darwinist control mechanisms.

Dr. Forrest Mims, who has been valiantly trying to expose Pianka's hideous calls, wrote to Pianka and asked for an explanation as to why he wanted to see a worldwide epidemic that would only kill Africans.

Pianka responded by saying he was not racially prejudice and wanted to see 90% of all races exterminated. As he puts it, 'He wants an equal opportunity killer virus.'

Dr. Mims rightfully concluded that, 'The only difference between Pianka and Hitler is that Hitler stated he wanted to kill five and a half *million* people, this guy is saying he wants to kill five and a half *billion* people.'[1]

Now folks, how many of you would like to have that guy as your teacher? You'd learn real fast not to smart off to him, wouldn't you? But seriously, come on, can you believe what he's saying? He actually says annihilating 90% of the world's population is a good thing! Excuse me? And folks, it's one thing to think that, but here's my point. What did it say he was receiving his influence from? From Darwinian evolution, right? And folks, lest you think he's the only one being influenced like that, he's not alone. This deadly Darwinian influence is everywhere!

- Margaret Sanger called for, "The elimination of 'human weeds,' for the 'cessation of charity' because it prolonged the lives of the unfit, for the segregation of 'morons, misfits, and the maladjusted,' and for the sterilization of genetically inferior races."

- David Graber, a research biologist with the National Park Service said, "We have become a plague upon ourselves and upon the Earth...Until such time as homo sapiens should decide to rejoin nature, some of us can only hope for the right virus to come along."

- Jacques Cousteau wrote, "The damage people cause to the planet is a function of demographics – it is equal to the degree of development. One American burdens the earth much more than twenty Bangladeshes...This is a terrible thing to say. In order to stabilize world population, we must eliminate 350,000 people per day. It is a horrible thing to say, but it's just as bad not to say it."

- Bertrand Russell wrote, "At present the population of the world is increasing...War so far has had no great effect on this increase...I do not pretend that birth control is the only way in which population can be kept from increasing. There are others...If a Black Death could be spread throughout the world once in every generation, survivors could procreate freely without making the world too full...the state of affairs might be somewhat unpleasant, but what of it? Really high-minded people are indifferent to suffering, especially that of others."

- Dr. Sam Keen, a New Age writer and philosopher stated, "We must speak far more clearly about sexuality, contraception, about abortion, about values that control the population, because the ecological crisis, in short, is the population crisis. Cut the population by 90% and there aren't enough people left to do a great deal of ecological damage."

- Ted Turner said, "People who abhor the China one-child policy are dumb-dumbs. A total population of 250-300 million people, a 95% decline from present levels, would be ideal."[2]

Now folks, I don't know about you, but at this rate, hey, we need to stop calling evolution, evolution, and start calling it what it is. It's evilution, you know what I'm saying? It's spawning something alright, it's spawning death! And people, that's exactly why we're going to continue in our study, "The Witness of Creation." And so far we've seen the first three evidences of creation that God has left behind for us showing us that He's not just real, but that we really can have a personal intimate relationship with Him, the Creator of the universe was the evidences of An Intelligent Creation from very the Hand of Almighty God, as opposed to blind chance exploding from some sort of primeval blob, and then A Young Creation, as opposed to the long-age fairy tale time of evolution. And in the last five chapters we've saw how the third evidence was A Special Creation. And so far we've not only seen how the supposed evolution of people and animals and natural selection and embryology are a bunch of bologna, but in the last chapter we saw how mutations and vestigial organs are also a bunch a bologna. Why? Because they have some serious problems. Problems with the Theories, Problems with the Evidence, and Problems with the Quotes! Folks, they not only know it's a lie but they keep using these lies for evolution! And gee whiz folks, I got to thinking, man if all you've got are lies to support your theory, then maybe it's time to get a new theory, you know what I'm saying?

But you might be thinking, "Okay so maybe the supposed evolution of people and animals and all these mechanisms of evolution are a bunch of bologna, but what about the latest ones they've come up with. You know like **transitional fossils** and **punctuated equilibrium** where this is modern proof for evolution taking place? What about those? Well, hey, great question! But before we look at that, let's once again get acquainted with the Biblical answer for the existence of life.

Colossians 1:13-17 "For he has rescued us from the dominion of darkness and brought us into the kingdom of the Son he loves, in whom we have redemption, the forgiveness of sins. He is the image of the invisible God, the firstborn over all creation. For by him all things were created: things in heaven and on earth, visible and invisible, whether thrones or powers or rulers or authorities; all things were created by him and for him. He is before all things, and in him all things hold together."

Now folks, according to our text, the Bible is clear. Jesus is not only God in the flesh, but He's what? He also the One Who created all of flesh, right? From the visible to the invisible, from the heavens to the humans, right? But the problem is, what does evolution teach? Do they say, "Oh yeah, Jesus created all things and even holds them together." Are you kidding? They say blind chance created all things and pure luck holds it together, right? Therefore, I'd say we better take a look at not just the Scriptural evidence but the scientific evidence of these latest theories of evolution and see just who's telling the truth, how about you? And we'll start with **transitional fossils**. Here's how the basic premise goes.

Evolutionists believe that over millions and billions of years there have been millions and billions of evolutionary changes in creatures. And they call each one of these supposed changes in a creature a "transition." And each one of these transitions is supposedly, slowly over time, changing the creature into a completely different kind of creature. And for proof, they say you can see evidence of this in the fossil record.

So my question is this? Is this really true? Are millions and billions of transitions over millions and billions of years what really brought life into being? Are you kidding? People, it's another evolutionary lie! How do I know? Because the **first reason** why we know Jesus created all of life is **Because Transitional Fossils are a Lie**! People, we're going to take a look at some serious problems with these supposed transitional fossils and you tell me if somebody's brain hasn't fossilized.

Problem of What We Find: Believe it or not, many evolutionists believe that the modern bat evolved over millions of years undergoing millions of transitions from a rat-like creature. In fact, the German name for bat is *"Fledermause"* which means "flying mice." But let's take a look at what we should expect to find if this transition from a rat to a bat where to have occurred.

Imagine for a moment we started off with one creature, the rat, and actually ended up with a new creature, the bat. First of all, stop and think about how many millions of supposed transitions there would have to be over millions of years to change from a rat to the bat. Therefore, of all the fossil remains, we should expect to find millions of these leftover remains of each of these millions of transitions, right?

However, the only problem is, that's not what we find! Out of the millions and billions of transitional fossils that should be there, there are none, zero, nada! That which should be the most in abundance is that which we do not find at all! Exactly opposite of what the theory of transitions imply!

Problem of What We See: It's bad enough that we do not find any of these supposed transitional fossils and what few they've tried to come up with like the horse and whale which we've already seen are completely phony, keep in mind the whole premise is that you start off with one unique creature that supposedly turns into a totally different creature altogether. However, the only problem is, that's not what we see!

For instance, take for example a **horseshoe crab** fossil from the supposed Ordovician Age said to be 450-million-year-old. Now, it was already demonstrated in the book **A Young Creation** that we've only been around for a few thousand years, but even giving the evolutionists their big dates, they've still got a huge problem. The problem is that this fossil is no different from horseshoe crabs today. Why haven't they long since transitioned into something else by now?

Or how about a **starfish** fossil touted by evolutionists to be 100 to 150 million years old. But guess what? It's the same as starfish today!

Or how about some **oyster** fossils said to be over 400 million years old. But again, they're no different than oysters today!

How about a supposed 1.9 million year old fossil **bacteria** from Western Ontario in Canada. The only problem is they have the same structures as bacteria living today.

Or consider the oldest known fossil **scorpion** found in East Kirkton in Scotland. This species is said to be 320 million years old but for some reason is still no different from today's scorpions.

Or how about an **insect** fossil in amber that was found on the Baltic Sea coast and dated by evolutionists at about 170 million years old. But for some reason, it's no different from its modern day counterparts.

How about a supposed 140 million year old **dragonfly** fossil found in Bavaria in Germany. Believe it or not, it's identical to dragonflies living today!

Or how about some supposed 35 million year old **flies**. But guess what? They have the same body structure as flies today.

Or how about a supposed 170 million year old fossil **shrimp** from the supposed Jurassic Age. But once again, it's no different from shrimp today.

Or consider the supposed 25 million year old **termite** fossils found in amber. Can you believe they're identical to termites living today?

Therefore, the point is this. If these creatures supposedly existed millions of years ago because of evolution then surely also because of evolution they would have made a transition into another creature by now, right? However, that's not what we see!

Out of the millions of fossil remains we do see, all we ever see are more of the same kind of creatures. Some may have gone extinct but none of them have ever turned into another kind! Exactly opposite of what the theory of transitions imply!

Problem of What We Hear:

1. Robert Carroll, an expert on vertebrate paleontology and a committed evolutionist, "Despite more than a hundred years of intense collecting efforts

since the time of Darwin's death, the fossil record still does not yield the picture of infinitely numerous transitional links that he expected."

2. Biologist Francis Hitching, "If we find fossils, and if Darwin's theory was right, we can predict what the rock should contain; finely graduated fossils leading from one group of creatures to another group of creatures at a higher level of complexity. But this is hardly ever the case. In fact, the opposite holds true.

   Darwin felt though that the "extreme imperfection" of the fossil record was simply a matter of digging up more fossils. But as more and more fossils were dug up, it was found that almost all of them, were very close to current living animals."

3. Stephen Jay Gould, a Harvard University paleontologist and well-known evolutionist, "The history of most fossil species include two features particularly inconsistent with gradualism: most species exhibit no directional change during their tenure on earth.

   They appear in the fossil record looking much the same as when they disappear. A species does not arise gradually by the steady transformation of its ancestors; it appears all at once and 'fully formed.'"

4. Niles Eldredge said, "That individual kinds of fossils remain recognizably the same throughout the length of their occurrence in the fossil record had been known to paleontologists long before Darwin published his *Origin*.

   One hundred and twenty years of paleontological research later, it has become abundantly clear that the fossil record will not confirm this part of Darwin's predictions. Nor is the problem a miserably poor record. The fossil record simply shows that this prediction is wrong."[3]

Now folks, I don't know about you, but I'd say based on the evidence we just saw, somebody's needs to make a "transition" all right. They need to make a transition to the brain cell center, you now what I'm saying? And gee, that would make evolution by way of transitional fossils a what? A lie! Shocker!

Oh, but that's not all. The **second reason** why we know Jesus created all of life is **Because Punctuated Equilibrium is a Lie**! People believe it or not, even after all we've seen, the evolutionists still will not admit defeat. No matter how many times they get caught making up stories, they just keep making up more stories! And one of the biggest ones to date is called Punctuated Equilibrium! And folks, all it is, is a fancy way of saying, "Okay, maybe the reason why we can't find any transitional fossils is because evolution didn't happen slowly over time but rapidly. Maybe it happened quickly in spontaneous burps!" For instance, "Maybe the first bird hatched from a reptile's egg!" And folks, I'm not making that up. That's really what this theory says!

So my question is this? Is Punctuated Equilibrium really true? Did a crocodile really give birth to a crow? Are you kidding? People, it's another evolutionary lie! We're going to take a look at some serious problems with this punctuated equilibrium thing and you tell me if somebody hasn't been punched one too many times!

Problem of Multiple Mutations: If punctuated equilibrium were to ever occur, then millions and billions of mutations have to suddenly occur all at once to produce a new and totally different "spontaneous" creature, like the bird hatching from a reptile's egg. However, what we observe is that if a mutation does occur, they are single and not multiple. If they occur, they happen one at a time, not millions at a time.

Problem of Beneficial Mutations: Not only would millions of mutation have to happen all at once if punctuated equilibrium were to ever occur, but keep in mind every single one of these mutation must be beneficial to the organism.

First of all, the odds of multiple mutations ever working together in harmony with all body parts simultaneously such as the body organs, bones, head, feet, DNA, and all the rest, are beyond reason! But secondly, as we've already seen, all we ever observe with mutations is that they are never beneficial but detrimental. They either hurt, harm, maim, or kill the creature. As one evolutionist put it, "These monsters are not 'hopeful' but 'hopeless.'

Problem of Time: Even if mutations were multiple and beneficial, even Stephen Jay Gould admitted that these "hopeful monsters" of punctuated equilibrium occur only every 50,000 years to help cover up the fact that they are not occurring today. But do the math on this.

One new species every 50,000 years would only yield 20 new species every 1 million years! But what we observe is that there are hundreds of thousands of plant and animal species on the earth. Therefore, all eternity itself could not provide enough time for all these creatures to spring forth!

Problem of Multiple Creatures: Even if mutations were multiple and beneficial and there was enough time for punctuated equilibrium to occur, keep in mind that two of these "spontaneous" events must occur simultaneously. This is because if this "new" creature is to survive, there must be one male and one female.

Then they have to appear on the scene close enough to find each other. Then they have to get interested in each other and hope the other one wants to marry them and have kids. And as if that wasn't a big enough feat, keep in mind what Gould said, that this rare event only happens once every 50,000 years. Question, "Who's going to wait around 50,000 before they get married and have kids let alone stay alive to have kids!!!"

Problem with the Evidence: Believe it or not, not only are there known problems with the theory of punctuated equilibrium but it is also known by the evolutionists that there is no evidence whatsoever to back it up.

For instance, Ernst Mayr, who's been called "The Dean of Darwinism," said, "To believe that such a drastic mutation would produce a viable new type is equivalent to believing in miracles. The finding of a suitable mate for the 'hopeless monster' and the establishment of reproductive isolation from the normal members of the parental population seem to me insurmountable difficulties."[4]

Now folks, I don't know about you, but I'd say based on the evidence we just saw, somebody's equilibrium needs to get "punctuated," all right. They need a serious dose of "laying on of hands" you know what I'm saying? And gee whiz, that would make evolution by way of punctuated equilibrium a what? A lie! Shocker!

Oh, but that's still not all. The **third reason** why we know Jesus created all of life is **Because Sequential Ordering is a Lie!** People, even if transitional fossils or punctuated equilibrium were true, and they're not, but even if they were, it still doesn't prove a thing! Why? Because stop and think about it! If you find a bone in the dirt, all you know about it is what? It died, right? You don't know anything else. You don't know if it had any kids let alone what kind of kids, right? Therefore, you can put any kind of bones in any kind of supposed sequential order you want but it still doesn't prove a thing! And to show you how goofy this sequential ordering really is, let's look at just a couple of problems with it.

Problem with Family Trees: The only problem with all those seemingly well-ordered evolutionary "family trees" in the textbooks is they're completely "out of order"! And not sequentially but in honesty! Believe it or not, all these so-called transitional family trees cited as "visual" proof for evolution are not only pure poppycock, they're admitted as such by the evolutionists.

For instance, even evolutionist Stephen Jay Gould said, "The evolutionary trees that adorn our textbooks have data only at the tips and nodes of their branches; the rest is inference, however reasonable, not the evidence of fossils." And evolutionist Mary Leakey said, "All of those trees of life with the branches of our ancestors – that's a lot of nonsense!"

And finally, in an article in the leading journal *Science*, "In the years after Darwin, his advocates hoped to find predictable progressions. In general these have not been found yet the optimism has died hard, and some pure fantasy has crept into textbooks."

Problem with the Whole Idea: To put the nail in the coffin so to speak with this whole idea of sequential ordering, listen to this humorous analogy revealing how there's no way this "ordering of bones" can be used as proof for evolution. As you will see, sequential ordering is so bogus that you can use it to create the so-called evolution of just about anything, including plastic silverware. He says:

"Just because you can arrange animals in a certain order doesn't prove a thing. Even if you find them buried in a certain order, that doesn't prove a thing. If I get buried on top of a hamster, does that prove he's my grandpa?

I've been doing a lot of research on the evolution of the fork. I've pieced together fragmentary evidence for years. I believe after intensive research, the knife evolved first and then slowly evolved into the spoon. It took millions of years with great geological pressures that squeezed, dished it out and widened it up a little bit. And then slowly, erosion cut grooves into the end and turned it into the short tine fork. And then very slowly over millions of years, the grooves got longer and wider until it turned into the long tine fork.

I knew I had the right order, but I felt like I had a missing link, particularly between spoons and forks. You see, spoons are rounded and have no grooves but forks are squared and grooved. That's two jumps in one. Even punctuated equilibrium can't do that. So I knew I had a missing link but I couldn't find it.

Until one day I'm flying in an airplane on US Air, 30,000 feet off the ground, and a stewardess walked down the isle, and handed me the missing link! I don't think she knew what she had. But my trained scientific eye picked it up. I said, 'This is it!' Then later that day I went to get some chicken for lunch and found another one. There they are folks, the missing links…sporks!

So now the evolution of silverware is becoming complete. All I need to do is apply for a 10 million dollar grant and I think I can wrap this up. I've found a lot of evidence since then. I've been gathering data on this for a long time. I've even found some mutants along the way (melted plastic forks). They didn't quite make it for some reason.

You know, it was very interesting though. As soon as people found out that I was doing research on the evolution on the fork, everybody wanted to become famous. They sent me all their data from all over the country. Even some lies got sent to me. One of them was an obvious fake. It was a fork head on a spoon handle. It didn't get by me though. This is a cutthroat business, this fossil business is dangerous you know, you have to watch them. But I caught it right away. It's not in my museum. The rest of them are though.

Now look, you can arrange letters in order and try to prove something if you want. You can turn a cat to a cot to a dot to a dog making one letter change at a time. If you play around for a while, you can turn yourself into a fool. Doesn't take long either!"[5]

Now how many of you are going to take a closer look at your silverware today when you go out to lunch? Hey, you might find a missing link alright, maybe it's a piece of sausage on the end of your fork! In fact, I was thinking about messing with the evolutionist's minds by having my wife bury me on top of my two wiener dogs. Boy, that'd mess them up, wouldn't it? Hopefully she'd do it after I'm dead. But seriously as you can see, even if all that other stuff about a gradual or rapid evolution were true, and it's not, the whole premise of sequential ordering still doesn't prove a thing, does it? Not at all! In fact, Charles Darwin actually said:

"If it could be demonstrated that any complex organism existed which could not possibly have been formed by numerous, successive, slight modifications, my theory would absolutely break down."

And folks, I don't know about you, but I'd say based upon what we've seen in this chapter let alone the last five, I'd say ol' Charlie's theory of evolution, has just what? By his own admission it just broke down, didn't it?

But you might be thinking, "Okay so maybe all these supposed evolutionary mechanisms for the existence of life are a bunch of bologna and holds no bearing on A Special Creation but speaking of life, this means that the only option then, is that God has to be the Author of life. But if the Genesis account of God being the Creator of all life really can be taken literally as we've seen through the evidences of An Intelligent Creation, A Young Creation, and A Special Creation, then does that mean we can also take literally the Genesis account of God judging the whole world with a worldwide flood for their wickedness? I mean, did a guy named Noah and his family really exist let alone really build an actual giant ark that housed two of every kind of creature on the earth enabling them to survive a global catastrophe? Well hey, great question! I guess that's why we're going to begin a new section called, A Judged Creation: In the Days of Noah. Did God really judge the whole world with a global flood and only save those who got into His boat? And more importantly, is God really going to judge the world again, this time with a global firestorm, and only those who get into His Son will be saved? I guess we'll get to that in the next book!

How to Receive Jesus Christ:

1. Admit your need (I am a sinner).

2. Be willing to turn from your sins (repent).

3. Believe that Jesus Christ died for you on the Cross and rose from the grave.

4. Through prayer, invite Jesus Christ to come in and control your life through the Holy Spirit. (Receive Him as Lord and Savior.)

What to pray:

Dear Lord Jesus,

I know that I am a sinner and need Your forgiveness. I believe that you died for my sins. I want to turn from my sins. I now invite You to come into my heart and life. I want to trust and follow You as Lord and Savior.

In Jesus' name. Amen.

Notes

Chapter 17 *The Lie of the Ape Men*

1. *Story of Scope Monkey Trial*
   (http://www.counterbalance.net/history/scopes-body.html)
   (http://www.fillthevoid.org/Creation/Hovind/Brainwashed.html)
2. *Behavior Statistics*
   (http://www.linda.net/graphs.html)
   (http://www.algonet.se/~tourtel/hovind_seminar/seminar_part1a.html)
   (http://www.geocities.com/Heartland/Village/8759/youth-stats.html)
   (http://www.biblesabbath.org/bacchiocchi/endtimewickedness.html)
   (http://www.seebo.net/crisis.html)
3. *How Evolutionists Say Man was Created*
   (http://www.middletownbiblechurch.org/manchris/manchr1.htm)
   "The Awesome Worlds Within a Cell," National Geographic, September,
   1976, pp. 392-393)
   "Evolution" by Ruth Moore published by TIME Incorporated (TIME-LIFE
   series), 1964, pp.109-116).
4. *Ape Men Myths*
   (http://www.straight-talk.net/evolution/misslinks.htm)
   (http://www.christiananswers.net/q-eden/edn-c008.html)
   (http://www.algonet.se/~tourtel/hovind_seminar/seminar_part2.html)
   (http://www.christianity.gr/ef_ag/2001/july_august/sci.htm)
   (http://www.geocities.com/johnh_vanbc/bible/mythed.html)
   (http://www.nwcreation.net/evolutionfraud.html)
   (http://emporium.turnpike.net/C/cs/evid4.htm)
   (http://www.fillthevoid.org/Creation/Hovind/Brainwashed.html)
   (http://www.alexfound.org/creation/dewitt/hoaxes.htm)
   (http://www.wasdarwinright.com/Earlyman.asp)
   (http://emporium.turnpike.net/C/cs/evid5.htm)
   (http://emporium.turnpike.net/C/cs/evid6.htm)
   (http://www.darwinismrefuted.com/origin_of_man.html)
5. *Quotes Debunking Ape Men Myth*
   (http://emporium.turnpike.net/C/cs/evid4.htm)

(http://emporium.turnpike.net/C/cs/bias.htm)
Kent Hovind, *Seminar Notebook*,
(Pensacola: Creation Science Evangelism, 2001, Pgs. 16,78)
Andrew Snelling, *The Revised Quote Book*,
(Acacia Ridge: Answers in Genesis, 1990, Pgs. 14,16)
6. *Quote Martin Luther*
Kent Hovind, *Seminar Notebook*,
(Pensacola: Creation Science Evangelism, 2001, Pg. 4)

Chapter 18 *The Lie of Horse & Whale Evolution*

1. *Quote New Politically Correct Bible*
Ravi Zacharias, *Deliver Us From Evil*
(Dallas: Word Publishing, 1996, Pgs. 52-53)
2. *Quote New Feminist Bible*
(http://www.worldnetdaily.com/news/printer-friendly.asp?ARTICLE_ID
=44563)
3. *Quote New Evolution Bible*
(http://www.worldnetdaily.com/news/article.asp?ARTICLE_ID=54518)
4. *Evolution's Version of the Horse*
(http://www.christiananswers.net/q-aig/aig-c016.html)
(http://www.gluhm.com/Pages/Evolution/How%20works.htm)
(http://www.talkorigins.org/faqs/horses/horse_evol.html)
5. *Problems with Horse Evolution*
(http://www.darwinismrefuted.com/natural_history_2_12.html)
(http://www.christiananswers.net/q-aig/aig-c016.html)
(http://www.algonet.se/~tourtel/hovind_seminar/seminar_part4b.html)
(http://www.fillthevoid.org/Creation/Hovind/Brainwashed.html)
(http://www.angelfire.com/mi/dinosaurs/horse.html)
Kent Hovind, *Seminar Notebook*,
(Pensacola: Creation Science Evangelism, 2001, Pg. 5)
6. *Evolution's Version of the Whale*
(http://www.environment.sa.gov.au/coasts/whales/biol.html)
(http://www.apologeticspress.org/docsdis/2002/dc-02-03.html)
(http://www.enchantedlearning.com/subjects/whales/allabout/Evol.shtml)
(http://www.pbs.org/wgbh/evolution/library/03/4/l_034_05.html)
7. *Problems with Whale Evolution*
(http://www.darwinismrefuted.com/natural_history_2_15.html)

(http://www.answersingenesis.org/home/area/re1/chapter5.asp)
(http://www.algonet.se/~tourtel/hovind_seminar/seminar_part4b.html)
(http://www.apologeticspress.org/docsdis/2002/dc-02-03.html)
(http://www.talkorigins.org/features/whales/)
(http://www.icr.org/pubs/imp/imp-304.htm)
(http://www.answersingenesis.org/creation/v19/i1/whales.asp)
(http://www.answersingenesis.org/creation/v23/i4/almostwhale.asp)

Chapter 19 *The Lie of Natural Selection*

1. *Story of Adolph Hitler*
   (http://auschwitz.dk/Hitler.htm)
   (http://www.crystalinks.com/hitler.html)
2. *Hitler's Hit List*
   (http://www.acts2.com/thebibletruth/Evolution_Hitlers_Racist_Theories.
   htm)
3. *How Natural Selection is Supposed to Work*
   (http://www.pathlights.com/ce_encyclopedia/09nsel04.htm)
   (http://www.open2.net/nextbigthing/evolution/evolution_in_depth/in_dep(th.
   htm#natural)
   (http://www.cryingvoice.com/Evolution/NaturalSelection.html)
   (http://www.knowledgerush.com/kr/encyclopedia/Natural_selection/)
   (http://www.pathlights.com/ce_encyclopedia/20hist02.htm)
4. *Problems with the Process of Natural Selection*
   (http://www.cryingvoice.com/Evolution/NaturalSelection.html)
   (http://www.fillthevoid.org/Creation/Hovind/Brainwashed.html#
   peppered)
   (http://www.pathlights.com/ce_encyclopedia/09nsel02.htm)
   .(http://www.pathlights.com/ce_encyclopedia/09nsel03.htm)
   (http://www.bluediamond.com/almonds/process/growers.cfm)
   (http://www.satake.co.uk/noflash.html)
   (http://cvm.msu.edu/courses/AP/bessie/breeds/breeds.htm)
   (http://www.akc.org/breeds/recbreeds/breeds_a.cfm)
5. *Problems with the Examples of Natural Selection*
   (http://www.trueauthority.com/cvse/moth.htm)
   (http://www.trueorigin.org/pepmoth1.asp)
   (http://www.apologeticspress.org/inthenews/2003/itn-03-36.htm)
   (http://www.exchangedlife.com/Creation/pepper.shtml)

(http://www.cryingvoice.com/Evolution/NaturalSelection.html)
(http://www.fillthevoid.org/Creation/Hovind/Brainwashed.html)
(http://www.alexfound.org/creation/dewitt/hoaxes.htm)
(http://www.darwinismrefuted.com/mechanisms04.html)
(http://www.pathlights.com/ce_encyclopedia/09nsel03.htm)
(http://www.pathlights.com/ce_encyclopedia/09nsel05.htm)

6. *Quotes of Evolutionists Admitting Problems with Natural Selection*
   (http://www.pathlights.com/ce_encyclopedia/09nsel04.htm)
7. *Problems with the Belief of Natural Selection*
   (http://emporium.turnpike.net/C/cs/hssodar.htm)
   (http://evolution-facts.org/c19b.htm)

Chapter 20 *The Lie of Embryology*

1. *Story of Ota Benga*
   (http://emporium.turnpike.net/C/cs/hsota.htm)
   (http://www.answersingenesis.org/Home/Area/oneblood/chapter10.asp)
2. *How Embryology is Supposed to Work*
   (http://www.christiananswers.net/q-eden/edn-c024.html)
   (http://www.alexfound.org/creation/dewitt/hoaxes.htm)
   (http://www.nwcreation.net/evolutionfraud.html)
   (http://www.creationism.org/caesar/haeckel.htm)
   (http://www.sermonaudio.com/new_details.asp?8360)
   (http://www.apologeticspress.org/rr/rr1994/r&r9409b.htm)
   (http://www.apologeticspress.org/docsdis/2001/dc-01-06.htm)
   (http://www.answersingenesis.org/creation/v18/i2/haeckel.asp)
3. *Problems with the Theory of Embryology*
   (http://www.christiananswers.net/q-eden/edn-c024.html)
   (http://www.apologeticspress.org/rr/rr1994/r&r9409a.htm)
   (http://www.darwinismrefuted.com/embryology_04.html)
   (http://www.algonet.se/~tourtel/hovind_seminar/seminar_part4a.html)
   (http://www.pathlights.com/ce_encyclopedia/17rec01.htm)
4. *Problems with the Evidence of Embryology*
   (http://www.fillthevoid.org/Creation/Hovind/Brainwashed.html)
   (http://www.christiananswers.net/q-eden/edn-c024.html)
   (http://www.nwcreation.net/evolutionfraud.html)
   (http://www.sermonaudio.com/new_details.asp?8360)
   (http://strengthsandweaknesses.org/news.10.01.2003.htm)

(http://www.apologeticspress.org/rr/rr1994/r&r9409a.htm)
(http://www.apologeticspress.org/docsdis/2001/dc-01-06.htm)
(http://www.apologeticspress.org/docsdis/2001/dc-01-06.htm)
(http://www.darwinismrefuted.com/embryology_04.html)
(http://www.answersingenesis.org/creation/v18/i2/haeckel.asp)
5. *Quotes of Evolutionists Admitting Problems with Embryology*
(http://www.creationism.org/caesar/haeckel.htm)
(http://www.sermonaudio.com/new_details.asp?8360)
(http://www.apologeticspress.org/docsdis/2001/dc-01-06.htm)
(http://www.apologeticspress.org/rr/rr1994/r&r9409a.htm)
6. *Quotes on Embryology Being Used to Justify Abortion*
(http://www.christiananswers.net/q-eden/edn-c024.html)
(http://www.apologeticspress.org/rr/rr1994/r&r9409b.htm)
(http://www.apologeticspress.org/docsdis/2001/dc-01-06.htm)
7. *Abortion Statistics*
(http://www.algonet.se/~tourtel/hovind_seminar/seminar_part4a.html)
Whistleblower Magazine, (Vol. 12 No. 1, January 2003, Pg.11)

Chapter 21 *The Lie of Mutations and Vestigial Organs*

1. *Story of Aborigine Skulls*
(http://www.harunyahya.com/disasters03.php)
(http://www.macha.free-online.co.uk/ausrace.html)
(http://www.answersingenesis.org/home/area/OneBlood/chapter9.asp)
2. *Evolution's Version of Mutations*
(http://www.pathlights.com/ce_encyclopedia/10mut05.htm)
(http://www.pathlights.com/ce_encyclopedia/10mut10.htm)
(http://www.pathlights.com/ce_encyclopedia/10mut02.htm)
3. *Problems with the Theory of Mutations*
(http://www.pathlights.com/ce_encyclopedia/10mut05.htm)
(http://www.pathlights.com/ce_encyclopedia/10mut06.htm)
(http://www.pathlights.com/ce_encyclopedia/10mut10.htm)
(http://www.algonet.se/~tourtel/hovind_seminar/seminar_part4a.html)
(http://www.pathlights.com/ce_encyclopedia/10mut02.htm)
(http://www.pathlights.com/ce_encyclopedia/10mut03.htm)
(http://www.pathlights.com/ce_encyclopedia/10mut11.htm)
(http://www.darwinismrefuted.com/mechanisms06.html)
4. *Problems with the Examples of Mutations*

(http://www.pathlights.com/ce_encyclopedia/10mut05.htm)
(http://www.pathlights.com/ce_encyclopedia/10mut10.htm)
(http://www.christiananswers.net/q-eden/genetic-mutations.html)
(http://www.pathlights.com/ce_encyclopedia/10mut03.htm)
(http://www.pathlights.com/ce_encyclopedia/10mut11.htm)
(http://www.darwinismrefuted.com/embryology_01.html)
5. *Quotes of Evolutionists Admitting Problems with Mutations*
    (http://www.pathlights.com/ce_encyclopedia/10mut05.htm)
    (http://www.pathlights.com/ce_encyclopedia/10mut06.htm)
    (http://www.darwinismrefuted.com/mechanisms06.html)
6. *Evolution's Version of Vestigial Organs*
    (http://www.pathlights.com/ce_encyclopedia/16vest01.htm)
    (http://www.apologeticspress.org/docsdis/2001/dc-01-07.htm)
    (http://www.apologeticspress.org/rr/rr1994/r&r9409a.htm)
    (http://www.darwinismrefuted.com/embryology_02.html)
    (http://www.darwinismrefuted.com/mechanisms06.html)
7. *Problems with the Theory of Vestigial Organs*
    (http://www.algonet.se/~tourtel/hovind_seminar/seminar_part4b.html)
    (http://www.pathlights.com/ce_encyclopedia/16vest01.htm)
    (http://www.pathlights.com/ce_encyclopedia/16vest02.htm)
    (http://www.apologeticspress.org/docsdis/2001/dc-01-07.htm)
    (http://www.darwinismrefuted.com/embryology_02.html)
8. *Problems with the Examples of Vestigial Organs*
    (http://www.algonet.se/~tourtel/hovind_seminar/seminar_part4b.html)
    (http://www.pathlights.com/ce_encyclopedia/16vest01.htm)
    (http://www.pathlights.com/ce_encyclopedia/16vest02.htm)
    (http://www.apologeticspress.org/docsdis/2001/dc-01-07.htm)
    (http://www.fillthevoid.org/Creation/Hovind/Brainwashed.html)
    (http://www.apologeticspress.org/rr/rr1994/r&r9409a.htm)
    (http://www.darwinismrefuted.com/embryology_02.html)
9. *Quotes of Evolutionists Admitting Problems with Vestigial Organs*
    (http://www.pathlights.com/ce_encyclopedia/16vest02.htm)
    (http://www.apologeticspress.org/docsdis/2001/dc-01-07.htm)
    (http://www.darwinismrefuted.com/embryology_02.html)

Chapter 22 *The Lie of Fossil Transitions*

1. *Story of Dr. Eric Pianka*

(http://www.infowars.com/articles/life/pianka_kill_90_percent_echos_un_elite_ngo_policies.htm)
2. *Quotes on Population Control*
(http://www.radioliberty.com/pca.htm)
(http://sophrosyne.radical.r30.net/wordpress/?p=965)
3. *Problems with Transitional Fossils*
(http://science.howstuffworks.com/bat1.htm)
(http://www.icr.org/pubs/imp/imp-095.htm)
(http://www.darwinismrefuted.com/origin_of_species_05.html)
(http://www.darwinismrefuted.com/origin_of_species_06.html)
(http://www.angelfire.com/mi/dinosaurs/livingfossils.html)
(http://www.darwinismrefuted.com/origin_of_species_04.html)
4. *Problems with Punctuated Equilibrium*
(http://www.darwinismrefuted.com/equilibrium_02.html)
(http://www.darwinismrefuted.com/origin_of_species_06.html)
(http://www.pathlights.com/ce_encyclopedia/10mut03.htm)
(http://www.pathlights.com/ce_encyclopedia/10mut14.htm)
5. *Problems with Sequential Ordering*
Andrew Snelling, *The Revised Quote Book*,
(Acacia Ridge: Answers in Genesis, 1990, Pg. 10)
(http://www.algonet.se/~tourtel/hovind_seminar/seminar_part4b.html)
(http://www.darwinismrefuted.com/origin_of_species_06.html)

Chapter 23 *The Evidence of a Global Catastrophe*

1. *The Biblical Account of the Seven Year Tribulation*
(Summarized by Billy Crone from the Book of Revelation)
2. *The Evidence of Logic*
(http://www.answersingenesis.org/Home/Area/AnswersBook/global10.asp)
(http://www.answersingenesis.org/creation/v21/i3/flood.asp)
(http://christiananswers.net/q-eden/edn-c005.html)
(http://genesis.amen.net/history.html)
(http://www.creationevidence.org/scientific_evid/evidencefor/evidencefor.html)
(http://genesis.amen.net/earth.html)
(http://www.pathlights.com/ce_encyclopedia/05agee3.htm)

(http://www.drdino.com/QandA/index.jsp?varFolder=CreationEvolution&varPage=UniverseIsNotBillionsofYearsOld.jsp)
(http://www.christiancourier.com/archives/babel.htm)
Kent Hovind, *Seminar Notebook*,
(Pensacola: Creation Science Evangelism, 2001, Pg. 13)

3. *The Evidence of Language*
   (http://www.christiancourier.com/articles/read/the_tower_of_babel_legend_or_history)
   (http://www.answersingenesis.org/home/area/feedback/2006/1027.asp)
   (http://www.answersingenesis.org/creation/v15/i3/ripley.asp)
   Kent Hovind, *Seminar Notebook*,
   (Pensacola: Creation Science Evangelism, 2001, Pg. 13)
   (http://www.answersingenesis.org/tj/v13/i2/genesis.asp)
   (http://www.answersingenesis.org/articles/am/v3/n2/four-women-boat-kids)
   (http://s8int.com/noahsark12.html)
   (http://s8int.com/phile/noahsark24.html)
   (http://www.answersingenesis.org/tj/v12/i1/eve.asp)
   (http://evolution-facts.org/Ev-V2/2evlch19a.htm)
   (http://www.pathlights.com/ce_encyclopedia/Encyclopedia/14flod04.htm)

4. *The Evidence of Lineage*
   Kent Hovind, *Seminar Notebook*,
   (Pensacola: Creation Science Evangelism, 2001, Pg. 13)
   (http://www.answersingenesis.org/creation/v22/i1/peleg.asp)
   (http://www.answersingenesis.org/tj/v13/i2/genesis.asp)
   (http://www.answersingenesis.org/articles/am/v3/n2/four-women-boat-kids)
   (http://s8int.com/noahsark12.html)
   (http://s8int.com/phile/noahsark24.html)
   (http://www.answersingenesis.org/tj/v12/i1/eve.asp)
   (http://evolution-facts.org/Ev-V2/2evlch19a.htm)
   (http://www.pathlights.com/ce_encyclopedia/Encyclopedia/14flod04.htm)

5 *The Evidence of Legend*
   (http://www.pathlights.com/ce_encyclopedia/Encyclopedia/14flod02.htm)
   (http://evolution-facts.org/Evolution-handbook/E-H-14a.htm)
   (http://creationwiki.org/Flood_legends)
   (http://evolution-facts.org/Ev-V2/2evlch19a.htm)
   (http://www.answersingenesis.org/articles/am/v2/n2/flood-legends)

(http://members.aol.com/adobebill/E_Flood.html)
(http://www.nwcreation.net/noahlegends.html)
(http://www.talkorigins.org/faqs/flood-myths.html)

Chapter 24 *The Evidence of a Great Fossilization*

1. *The Biblical Account of the Ten Plagues of Egypt*
   (http://www.essortment.com/all/tenplaguesofe_rwfp.htm)
2. *The Evidence of Sorted Layers*
   (http://www.nwcreation.net/geologycolumn.html)
   (http://www.godrules.net/evolutioncruncher/a19a.htm)
   (http://evolution-facts.org/Ev-V2/2evlch19a.htm)
   (http://evolution-facts.org/Evolution-handbook/E-H-14a.htm)
   (http://www.creationism.org/symposium/symp3no2.htm)
   (http://creationwiki.org/Flood_geology#Hydrological_sorting)
   (http://creationwiki.org/Hydrological_sorting)
   (http://creationwiki.org/Flood_geology#Hydrological_sorting)
   (http://cs.joensuu.fi/~vtenhu/hovind/CHP-5.htm)
   (http://www.creationscience.com/onlinebook/Liquefaction4.html)
   (http://www.answersingenesis.org/home/area/cfol/ch3-how-fast.asp)
   (http://www.pathlights.com/ce_encyclopedia/Encyclopedia/14flod08
   .htm)
   (http://www.creationism.org/symposium/symp3no2.htm)
3. *The Evidence of Sudden Death and Burial*
   (http://www.worldnetdaily.com/news/article.asp?ARTICLE_ID=56123)
   (http://evolution-facts.org/Ev-V2/2evlch19a.htm)
   (http://www.creationscience.com/onlinebook/LifeSciences25.html#
   wp1029340)
   (http://siriusknotts.wordpress.com/2008/09/08/darwins-dyke-what-the-
   fossil-record-actually-shows/)
   (http://www.bible.ca/tracks/rapid-fossils-ephemeral-markings.htm)
   (http://www.bible.ca/tracks/rapid-fossils-rapidly-perishing-detail-
   preserved.htm)
   (http://www.answersingenesis.org/home/area/cfol/ch3-how-fast.asp)
   (http://www.freewebs.com/trinitydefender/science.htm)
   (http://www.amnh.org/exhibitions/fightingdinos/ex-fd.html#)
4. *The Evidence of Swirling Graveyards*
   (http://thetruth.uv.ro/_books/_answ_book/Cap_04.html)

(http://cs.joensuu.fi/~vtenhu/hovind/CHP-5.htm)
(http://siriusknotts.wordpress.com/2008/09/08/darwins-dyke-what-the-fossil-record-actually-shows/)
(http://www.answersingenesis.org/home/area/cfol/ch3-how-fast.asp)
(http://www.s8int.com/boneyard1.html)
(http://www.s8int.com/boneyard2.html)
(http://www.s8int.com/boneyard3.html)
(http://www.s8int.com/boneyard5.html)
(http://www.bearfabrique.org/Catastrophism/floods/mfloods.html)
(http://evolution-facts.org/Appendix/a19a.htm)

5. *The Evidence of Super-sized Coal*
   (http://www.creationism.org/sthelens/MSH1b_7wonders.htm)
   (http://www.creationscience.com/onlinebook/HydroplateOverview3.html)
   (http://www.creationscience.com/onlinebook/Liquefaction5.html)
   (http://www.bible.ca/tracks/rapid-layers.htm)
   (http://www.s8int.com/boneyard6.html)
   (http://www.answersingenesis.org/creation/v6/i1/mtsthelens.asp)
   (http://evolution-facts.org/Ev-V2/2evlch19a.htm)
   (http://www.creationism.org/symposium/symp3no2.htm)
   (http://books.google.com/books?id=rP7wV9S1EsYC&pg=PA243&lpg=PA243&dq=blew+trees+into+spirit+lake&source=bl&ots=njy0yuckD-&sig=NnVnNYK7PKARrOeKiQadWkG5IBY&hl=en&ei=Vh92SoHdL461tgeG2pnMAQ&sa=X&oi=book_result&ct=result&resnum=4#v=onepage&q=blew%20trees%20into%20spirit%20lake&f=false)